Poppy Cooks

For

Nanny Vicky who always had me in the kitchen, peeling, chopping and learning the love that goes into food.

Dad, I can't remember much other than you teaching me to moonie. Just to let you know, it's still my party trick.

Wish you were both able to see this.

BLOOMSBURY PUBLISHING

Bloomsbury Publishing Plc
50 Bedford Square, London, WC1B 3DP, UK
29 Earlsfort Terrace, Dublin 2, Ireland

BLOOMSBURY, BLOOMSBURY PUBLISHING and the Diana logo
are trademarks of Bloomsbury Publishing Plc

First published in Great Britain 2021

A catalogue record for this book is available from the British Library

ISBN: HB: 978-1-5266-3923-3; eBook: 978-1-5266-3921-9

10 9 8 7 6 5 4 3 2 1

Project Editor: Judy Barratt
Design and Art Direction: AOTA.studio
Photographer: Louise Hagger
Food Stylist: Poppy O'Toole
Prop Stylist: Alexander Breeze
Indexer: Hilary Bird

Printed and bound in Germany by Mohn Media

To find out more about our authors and books visit
www.bloomsbury.com and sign up for our newsletters

Poppy Cooks
The Food You Need

Learn the basics. Up your cooking game.
Delicious food every time.

BLOOMSBURY PUBLISHING
LONDON · OXFORD · NEW YORK · NEW DELHI · SYDNEY

Contents

I've only gone and written a recipe book! 8
How this book works. 18
Recipe stuff. 21

Tomato Sauce 22

Core	A Labour of Love 24
Core	The Tomato Quickie 26
Staple	Well-good Meatballs 29
Brunch	Eggs Shakshuka'd 30
Potato	Popapas Bravas 33
Fancy AF	Chicken Parmigiana 34
Fancy AF	Aubergine Parmigiana 36

White Sauce 38

Core	Béchamel 40
Core	Cheese Sauce 42
Staple	Mac 'n' Cheese 44
Brunch	Mrs Croque 47
Potato	Bacon-y Garlic-y Potato-y 48
Fancy AF	Beef Shin Lasagne 50

Flat Bread 54

Core	Easy Flat Breads 56
Staple	Tikka Salmon 59
Brunch	Avo-bloomin-cado Brunch Wraps 60
Potato	Potato-topped Pizza Spud Breads 63
Fancy AF	Slow-roasted Harissa Lamb Shoulder 64

Emulsions 68

Core	Mayo 70
Core	Hollandaise 72
Staple	The Chicken Caesar 75
Brunch	Eggs Royale 76
Potato	Loaded Potato Salad 78
Fancy AF	Steak Béarnaise and Crunchy Roast Chips 80

Dressings 84

Core	Vinaigrette Dressing 87
Core	Cheese Dressing 88
Staple	Halloumi, Sweet Potato and Red Onion Salad 91
Brunch	The Breakfast Salad 92
Potato	Lemon-roasted Potatoes with Feta Dressing 96
Fancy AF	Buffalo Buttermilk Chicken with Blue Cheese Dressing 98

Batter Up 102

Core	Tempura Batter 104
Core	Beer Batter 106
Staple	Crispy Prawn Tacos with Sweetcorn Salsa 109
Brunch	Tempura Cabbage Fritters and Soy Dip 110
Potato	Potato Bhaji Butty 113
Fancy AF	The DIY Chippy Dinner 114

Savoury Pastry 118

Core	Shortcrust Pastry 120
Staple	Cheese and Onion Pie 122
Brunch	Brekkie Quiche 127
Potato	Bombay Potato Pasties 128
Fancy AF	Stroganoff Pie 132

Confit Garlic 136

Core	How to Confit Garlic 138
Staple	Greens Means Pasta 140
Brunch	Ain't Mushroom for Lunch 144
Potato	Garlic-buttered Crispy Gnocchi 146
Fancy AF	Chilli Garlic Prawns and Polenta 150

Up Your Roast 152

Core	Herb-roasted Chicken 156
Core	Apples 'n' Pears Pork 158
Core	Smoke and Stout Beef 160
Core	Red Onion Tarte Tatin 162
Staple	A Good Pork Stuffing 165
Potato	Potatoes Boulangère 166
Potato	Apple Mash 167
Potato	Roast Tatties 168
Staple	Yorkshire Puds 170
Fancy AF	Honey Parsnip Crumble 171
Fancy AF	Butter-roasted Carrots 173
Staple	Cauliflower Le Cheese 174
Fancy AF	Braised Red Cabbage 176

Sweet Pastry 180

Core	Sweet Pastry 182
Staple	Strawberry Tart 184
Brunch	Pop's Pop Tarts 188
Potato	Sweet Potato Pie 190
Fancy AF	Cherry Bakewell Cheesecake 194

Custard 198

Core	Perfect Custard 200
Staple	Butterscotch Apple Crumble 203
Brunch	Bananas and Custard French Toast 204
Potato	Custard Spudnuts 206
Fancy AF	Forget-the-Crème Brûlées 210

Meringue 212

Core	French Meringue 214
Core	Italian Meringue 216
Staple	Pat's Pav (On Tour) 218
Brunch	Eton Mess Pancakes 221
Potato	S'mores Dauphine 222
Fancy AF	Simply the Zest Lemon Meringue Pie 224

Index 228
I say potato... 234
Thank You 239
About Poppy 240

I've only gone and written a recipe book!

I've thought about my first recipe book for a LONG TIME! Lots of little girls plan their weddings with scrapbooks and mood boards, but ten-year-old Poppy was instead thinking what her cook book would be like... and now it's actually happened!

As a chef who loves to teach people about food, I've always wanted to make cooking accessible – and without the judgement. As a result of working your way through this book, I want you to find out (and then believe) that you can make incredible food. There are no scary recipes that you'll look at and think: 'How on earth am I meant to do that?!' Sure, you might make a few mistakes along the way – but, who cares? You'll learn from them, keep going and definitely have a plateful of deliciousness by the end of it. And I can guarantee that, together, we'll have fun in the process.

I've been working in kitchens for over a decade and I still make mistakes (shout-out to that time I poured a pork sauce that my boss had taken two days to make down the sink because I thought it was old caramel). And to be fair to me, I've seen chefs at every level make a lot of mistakes... but maybe I just made a few more as an often-distracted chef who spent too much time bellowing Britney to lighten the mood in a stressful kitchen. When did cooking stop being fun? Yes, we all want to avoid messing up, but how can we learn if we don't take risks?

So, make mistakes. They are good for you. Every mistake is part of the process of getting to know how you-the-chef likes to cook, and finding out what's special about you-the-creator

and how you can make food that you love every day. We're not just talking about a few dishes you want to make sometimes – we're dealing with the amazing food you need *every day*.

It's easy to feel intimidated by gorgeous food. I don't know about anyone else, but I used to see the perfect photos on Instagram and think: 'There's no way I'm going to be able to place my banana on my baked oats to look that edgy.' Let's just take a moment of silence for the endless food photos I've taken and have never uploaded, even as a professional chef. Sliding up the saturation and brightness can't always work miracles.

But that's where I see food differently. Food for me is love – it's not perfection. Food is my Nan's bolognese at the end of the week, as the members of my family made their way through a bottle of red wine (or six) and an eight-year-old me planned how I'd get away from the table to grab some pre-dessert from the fridge before actual dessert came out. It's the giant paella that I tripled in size during catering lessons so that I could make my mates feel like we were the coolest kids in school as we all tucked into it in the lunch hall instead of the usual Pasta King tub. This book is all about the food you love and how, together, we can make sure you're eating it every day.

A bit about me

My love of food began at a young age because I loved eating. And I loved eating A LOT. It wasn't long before I clocked that if I offered to help in the kitchen, there would be more chances to eat along the way. (Not much has changed, to be fair. Even now my whole day revolves around food and when or what I'll be eating next.)

I spent a lot of time cooking with my Nan, between watching Keith Floyd on the TV in a living room surrounded by recipe books. My Nan loved recipe books, a love that she passed on to my Mom and then to me – and now (a bit surreally, to be honest) I have my own recipe book. My Nan sadly passed away when I was just ten, but the memory of how food (especially her

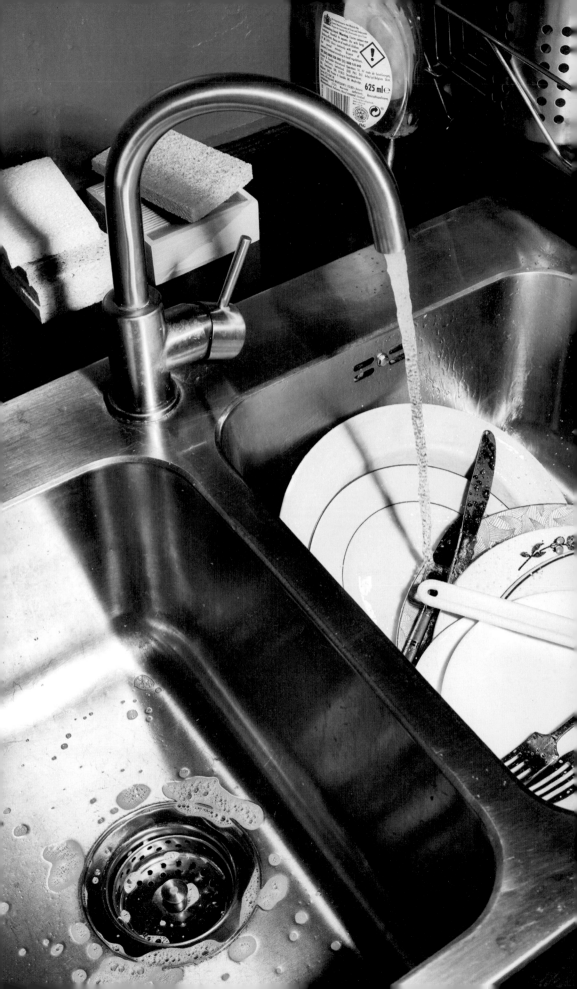

food) can make you feel so good inspires me to teach as many people as I can to cook.

In all honesty, I was rubbish at school. I just was never committed enough to follow anything through to the end. (Let's hope you don't get halfway through the book and realise it's unfinished... .) In my teens, I didn't commit to pushing my love of cooking, either: I entered a Future Chef competition at school aged 15 and by some complete fluke, I won. But, then I dropped out of the regional rounds because I was meant to practise after school twice a week to refine my craft... but the pull of sitting at home glued to MSN for eight hours won out instead.

Nonetheless, at this point I did at least realise I could cook well. I started working as a waitress at a local restaurant and soon convinced the chef to let my inexperienced self help out in the kitchen. It was a Scotch-eggs-and-poached-pears kinda vibe (not together), but it was a huge step up from the other job I was working at the same time: a chef at a local care home, where I made corned beef hash and endless cups of tea, with *The Chase* constantly on the TV. (The residents loved it.)

I should say that these two jobs were on top of school. Make no mistake, though, the two jobs were for no other reason than they gave me an excuse not to do coursework or revision, and justified why I left school having failed my A levels. Well, not entirely failed: I got a D in Food Tech, which I think is actually classed as a pass (or at least I've told myself that since). This is where I should say that school is very important – but it really isn't for everyone. School isn't the reason that in the last year I've achieved some of my goals and dreams – that's because at age 19, I kicked into fifth gear and worked my socks off. So, what I will say is: it's never too late to start again and to keep pushing.

And that was when I came across an apprenticeship at a Michelin-starred restaurant in Birmingham. I definitely felt too old for it – all my friends were off at uni and here I was applying for a £3-an-hour job to go back to college with students two or more years younger than I was. The apprenticeship was like a 12-week college course/competition, at the end of which only

two of us would be chosen to carry on working in the restaurant. The course ended and two were chosen – neither of which was me. Luckily, though, the restaurant decided to pick a third, a wild card. Enter me, into the world of fine dining. Over time, I worked my way through all sorts of kitchens – from Michelin-starred to corporate catering – and I learnt exactly how to put incredible food on a plate.

You hear a lot of the same chat when you're a chef: 'What's it like to be a chef?' 'I bet your dinners at home are amazing!' 'Your family and friends are so lucky!' Reality check: your own dinners are rarely amazing. You'd be lucky to rush a supermarket meal deal between the 7am-to-5pm and 6pm-to-12am split shifts. And you're always washing it down with a Red Bull and embracing an evening of indigestion. On your days off? The priority is catching up on sleep rather than cooking more at home. That was my life for many years. I just got on with it.

Then, in March 2020, restaurants were forced to close because of the pandemic and I lost my job. But I started another crazy journey. I began making a few TikTok videos and here I am: millions of people have watched those videos and I have fallen in love with home cooking all over again. I have dedicated my career to learning the tricks of fine dining and how the industry works, but having the time at home has given me the opportunity to help people across the world bring everything I have learnt in professional kitchens to their own kitchen table.

Even now, saying 'millions of people'... there's a bit of me that's like, 'Shut up, Poppy. Stop bigging yourself up.' But my videos have had over 100 million views on TikTok... all while I've just been in my own kitchen during lockdowns, not seeing anyone, yet communicating with so many people every single day. Lots of you have shown me that you have a voice of doubt when you step into the kitchen, which tells you, 'I can't cook that', 'It's not worth me even trying' or 'Let's just order a takeaway.' But – and trust me when I say it – by the end of this book, I know you'll be creating some incredible dishes. Are you ready?

How this book works.

One thing I've learnt over the years is that there are crucial core recipes that can completely change the weekly shop. Nail those and breakfast, lunch and dinner become easy wins every day. That's the inspiration for the structure of this book and I want to use it to revolutionise how we look at food.

So, every chapter starts with a core recipe – from a tomato or béchamel sauce to perfect pastry and easy emulsions. The remaining recipes build on the core to give you meals from that one starting point. Each core isn't a one off, but a platform to create incredible dishes you might not have thought to try, but that you're totally capable of.

In each chapter, the recipes are:

The Core A fundamental recipe (sometimes two) that you can use in SO MANY ways for the rest of your life.

The Staple The go-to easy recipe using the Core. You'll want this one for dinner every week.

The Brunch The late-morning, early-afternoon filler that reinvents the Core to hit the spot on a lazy day.

The Potato My signature. It's no secret that I appreciate the versatility of a humble potato. Here, each Core finds its way into the eating of a potato for double-deliciousness.

The Fancy AF This recipe raises up the humble Core to create food that will blow your family and friends' socks off.

Once you start, you'll see that you can easily adapt each recipe based on your own tastes and preferences. Before you know it, you'll become a master creator in the kitchen.

1. Core

2. Staple

3. Brunch

4. Potato

5. Fancy AF

Recipe stuff.

I want these recipes to give you confidence – so you can think 'I don't have any of that, I'll use this instead.' Or, 'That's never enough for my HUNGER! I'll make more.' As a start, here's some know-how to help you get the most out of the recipes.

Serves I've given approximate servings, but let's face it, on a hungry day I'll eat half a cheese and onion pie to myself. Appetite is personal. Scale up or down as you see fit, just bear in mind that you might need to adjust the cooking times, too (see oven temperatures, below, for how to judge 'doneness').

Tablespoons and teaspoons That is measuring spoons, not eating spoons. Measure ingredients level unless I say heaped.

Herbs Unless I say to use dried, I mean fresh. Pack sizes vary, so a bunch means the smaller size (usually 20–25g/½–¾oz); a large bunch is closer to the big packs (about 40g/1½oz).

Salt Use fine salt, unless I specify flaky.

Butter Use whatever you have in your fridge, unless I specify unsalted. Taste for seasoning so that you don't over- or under-salt depending on which butter you've used.

Eggs Eggs are medium unless stated, and ideally free range.

Ingredient sizes Individual veg, fruit and eggs are assumed medium-sized, unless I've said to use large or small.

Oven temperatures Get to know your oven. What's hot in yours, might be a bit cooler or a bit hotter in mine. Use the cooking times as a guide, and then work with what you see, feel, taste and smell – I've always tried to give you a practical cue as to what you're looking for in a finished dish, as a guide.

One last thing If you're reading in **North America**, some of what I say may seem 'Eh?!' Flip to page 234 to translate. If you can, grab yourself a cheap set of at-home scales. We use them all the time in the UK – they save on having to wash up cups.

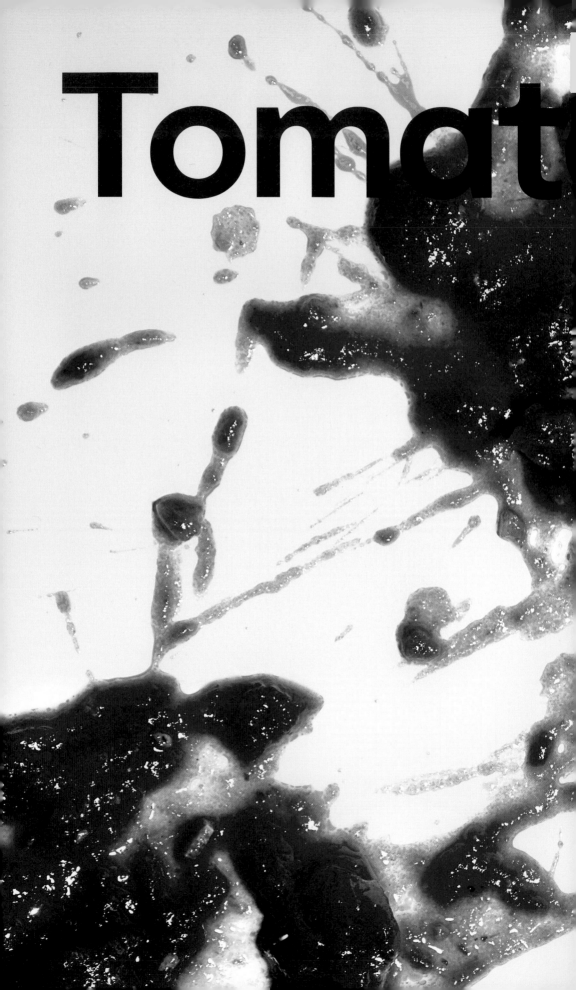

Tomat

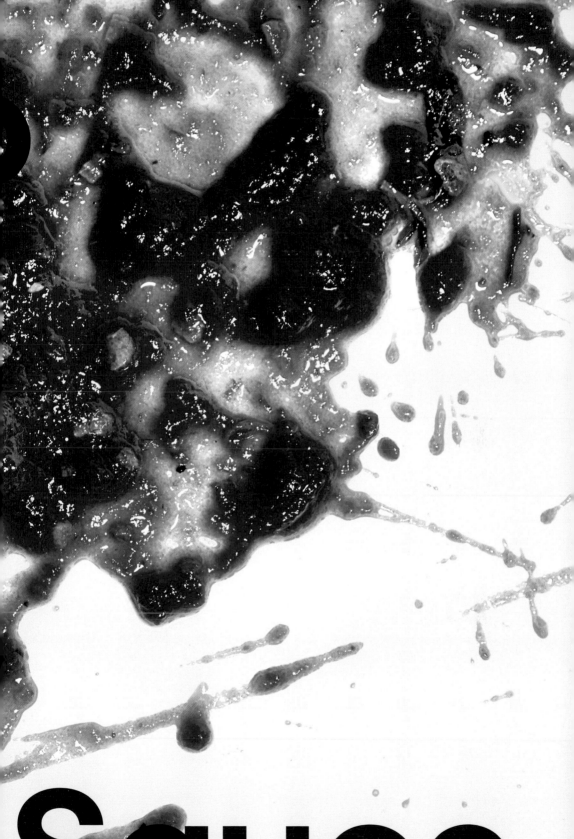

Sauce

A Labour of Love

It's true. I am in love with this tomato sauce. The cooking part takes a bit of time, but it is genuinely the easiest sauce you'll make and it's sooooo much better than any sauce you can pick up in a jar. Throw a load of ingredients into a pan, leave it over a low, slow heat for a few hours. The rest is history.

There are so many ways to use it – and not only in the recipes in this chapter. Get creative: make a meatball sandwich or a heartwarming pasta bake or even just use it as a base for greens and a pan-fried fillet of hake. The options are endless.

Serves 4–6 (depending on how you use it)

10 **garlic cloves**, peeled
1½ tsp **salt**, plus extra for the garlic
120ml/½ cup **olive oil**
6 x 400g/14oz tins of **plum tomatoes**
a big pinch of **black pepper**
2 tsp **sugar**
1 tsp **red wine vinegar**
a bunch of **basil**, leaves picked and torn
1 **red chilli** (optional), sliced into rounds (deseeded for less heat)

1. Mince your garlic into a paste: chop it as finely as you can, then sprinkle on a bit of salt (not the 1½ teaspoons, they are for later), then keep chopping and squashing with the blade of your knife. Alternatively, throw it in a garlic crusher with the bit of salt and you should be left with a lovely paste.

2. Place a large saucepan over a medium heat. Add the olive oil and garlic, like the match-made-in-heaven that they are.

3. Fry the garlic for about 2–3 minutes, until it's aromatic – you're not looking for any colour in the garlic.*TIP!

4. Add the tomatoes, then pour water into one of the empty tins and give it a swill. Transfer the water to the next empty tin, swill, then to the next and so on to get all of the tomato juice out. Add the tomato-y water to the pan, too.

5. Add the 1½ teaspoons of salt and the pinch of pepper, then reduce the temperature to low and leave the sauce to slowly bubble away for 2½ hours, until it's deep red and thick (it should reduce by about one quarter).

6. After the 2½ hours, stir through the sugar, vinegar and torn basil, and the chilli, if using, and you're ready to go. How easy was that?

*CHEF'S TIP
Be gentle with the garlic – you want it to soften without colouring. If you smell pungent, smoky garlic-ness, it's gone too far and is burning. Just peel some more and try again.

[STORAGE: FRIDGE **3 DAYS** / FREEZER **3 MONTHS**]

The Tomato Quickie

As much as I love the slow-cooked tomato goodness of A Labour of Love, let's be honest, we don't always have two hours to wait for that bubbling deliciousness. This version is for when you've got only 20 minutes – it's okay to have time for just a quickie if you're still left with a smile on your face.

Fast and efficient does the job (get your ingredients prepped before you start), and just wait until you taste its freshness – a punch that wins out over a jarred sauce every time.

Serves 4–6 (depending on how you use it)

- 1.4kg/3lb **cherry tomatoes**
- 120ml/½ cup **olive oil**
- 6 **garlic cloves**, peeled and chopped
- 1 **red onion**, peeled and finely chopped
- ½ bunch of **basil**, leaves picked and torn
- **salt** and **black pepper**

1. Using a large, sharp knife, slice all the tomatoes in half.*TIP!

2. Put a medium saucepan over a medium–high heat and add the olive oil.

3. Once the oil is hot, add about half the tomatoes so they instantly burst with all their gorgeous flavour.

4. Cook for about 5–7 minutes, stirring occasionally, until a thick juice starts forming, then add the garlic, onion and the remaining tomatoes.

5. Keep stirring, turn the heat down to medium, then taste and season.

6. Once the remaining tomatoes have softened (about 3–5 minutes), stir in the torn basil and remove the pan from the heat. This sauce is ready to use straight away, or leave it to cool and transfer it to an airtight container.

*CHEF'S TIP

I love this hack for cutting tomatoes all at once: put all the tomatoes in one layer on your work surface. Place the lid of an airtight container on the top. Hold the lid in place with your non-dominant hand, keeping the tomatoes steady underneath. Then, using the knife, cut under the lid through all the tomatoes in one go!

[STORAGE: FRIDGE **3 DAYS** / FREEZER **3 MONTHS**]

Well-good Meatballs

This is the 'I-made-that' pasta dish. It's your go-to dinner that'll hit all the right spots. The meatballs are all things beef Wellington, but in a ball (hence the 'well-good' name). They have everything you love about a meatball while incorporating rich-tasting mushrooms and being wrapped in pancetta.

Serves 2 (10–14 meatballs)

The core
½ recipe quantity of **tomato sauce** (see page 24 or 26)

For the well-good meatballs
2 tbsp **olive oil**
250g/9oz **closed-cup mushrooms**, finely chopped (or blitzed in a food processor)
2 **garlic cloves**, peeled and finely chopped
½ **onion**, peeled and finely chopped
2 **thyme sprigs**, leaves picked
250g/9oz **beef mince**
1 tbsp **Dijon mustard**
5–7 slices of **parma ham or prosciutto**, cut in half
1 tbsp **salt**, for the cooking water, plus extra to season
200g/7oz **dried spaghetti**
black pepper
plenty of **parmesan**, or any other cheese you fancy, grated, to serve

1. Preheat your oven to 200°C/180°C fan/400°F/Gas 6.

2. Put a large saucepan over a high heat and drizzle in the olive oil. Once hot, add the mushrooms and season with salt and pepper. Cook for about 2 minutes, or until the mushrooms are coloured. Reduce the heat to medium. Add the garlic, onion and thyme, then cook for about 10 minutes, until smelling lovely. Leave the mixture to cool slightly.

3. Tip the mince, mustard and cooled mushroom mixture into a bowl. Season with black pepper, then get your hands in there and mix it all together.

4. Heat a frying pan over a high heat. Fry 1 teaspoon of the mince mixture until cooked. Taste and adjust the seasoning of the mixture, if necessary.

5. Roll the mixture into 10–14 ping-pong-sized balls. Wrap 1 halved piece of parma ham or prosciutto around each ball, then place in a baking tray and bake for 25 minutes, until cooked through.

6. Meanwhile, fill a pan three-quarters full with water, add the tablespoon of salt and put the lid on. Place over a high heat and bring to the boil.

7. Just before the balls are ready, pour your tomato sauce into a large pan and warm it up. Add the cooked balls and keep warm over a low heat.

8. Cook the spaghetti in the boiling water until tender with a bit of bite (about 7–10 minutes). Transfer the pasta into the pan with the sauce and meatballs, along with a ladleful of the pasta water. (See tip, page 143.)

9. Twist and fold everything together, until you have a beautifully glossy and combined pasta dish! COVER IN ALL THE CHEEEEEESE!

Eggs Shakshuka'd

How do you like your eggs in the morning? Easy — shakshuka'd. If a shakshuka hasn't made its way to your regular brunch list, then it's time to change that. A beautifully baked egg, spiced tomato sauce with peppers, and with crusty bread to dip in — it's like egg and soldiers, except your egg's been sunbathing in a tomato-y beach of heaven. Perfection!

Serves 2

The core
½ recipe quantity of **tomato sauce** (see page 24 or 26)

For the shakshuka
½ tsp **chilli flakes**
1 tsp **fennel seeds**
½ tsp **ground cumin**
olive oil
1 **onion**, peeled and sliced
1 **red pepper**, deseeded and sliced
1 **yellow pepper**, deseeded and sliced
4 **eggs**
50g/2oz **feta**
salt and **black pepper**
a small bunch of **flat-leaf parsley**, leaves picked and chopped, to garnish
1 small loaf of **crusty bread**, to serve

1. Preheat the oven to 200°C/180°C fan/400°F/Gas 6.

2. Place a large, deep saucepan over a medium heat. Add the chilli flakes, fennel seeds and cumin and cook for about 4–5 minutes, until you can smell all the lovely scents of chilli and aniseed. Add enough olive oil to just cover the base of the pan and then add the tomato sauce.

3. Add the onion and both peppers to the pan, giving everything a good mix together, then leave to cook for 20 minutes, until the onion is cooked and the peppers are slightly softened.

4. Pour the contents of the pan into a trendy, ovenproof serving dish.

5. Using the back of a spoon, make 4 small wells in your sauce and crack an egg into each one. Season with salt and pepper.

6. Place the shakshuka into the oven (you can throw in the bread on the shelf below to warm up, if you like). Bake for about 15 minutes, until the egg whites are cooked but the yolks are still soft (or cook to your preference). Wayhayyy!

7. Crumble over your feta cheese, and sprinkle over your chopped parsley to garnish. Tear up your bread and dig in.

Popapas Bravas

I was a kid who spent summer on the beaches of Costa del Sol with a half-melting Maxibom washed down with a sandy Fanta Limón. Patatas bravas were a staple and have inspired this tomato-y potato creation. Emphasis here is on the word 'inspired' – this book promised potato dishes fresh from the mind of potato-lady Poppy Cooks, and this is exactly that.

Serves 2

The core
3–4 tbsp **tomato sauce** (see page 24 or 26)

For the popapas bravas
3 **maris piper potatoes**, cut into about 2cm/¾ inch cubes
1 tbsp **salt**, for the cooking water
4 tbsp **olive oil**
100g/3½oz **spicy chorizo**, peeled, and cut into nice, chunky chunks
1 tsp **smoked paprika**
1 tsp **sweet paprika**
50ml/3½ tbsp **chicken or vegetable stock**
1 recipe quantity of **Mayo** (see page 70), to serve (optional)
1 **garlic clove**, peeled (optional – minced into the mayo if using)

1. Preheat the oven to 220°C/200°C fan/425°F/Gas 7.

2. Put your spuds into a pan with the salt and cover with cold water. Bring to the boil over a high heat. Boil for 10 minutes or so, until the spuds are tender.

3. In this time, pour 3 tablespoons of the olive oil in a baking tray that will fit the potatoes and chorizo in a single layer. Place in the oven to get hot.

4. Once the potatoes are cooked, drain them in a colander, then suspend the colander in the potato pan and cover with a clean tea towel for about 5 minutes, until the potatoes have steamed off and dried out a bit.

5. Remove the hot baking tray from the oven and tip in the potatoes and the chorizo. Toss everything a bit to get it all coated in the fatty goodness.

6. Return the tray to the oven and roast the spuds and chorizo for 45 minutes, giving them a stir at 15-minute intervals, until the spuds are golden and the chorizo is crisp. (If you haven't already made your tomato sauce, you've got time for a Quickie while the potatoes are cooking.)

7. Meanwhile, place a frying pan over a medium heat and add the remaining olive oil. When hot, add both paprikas and sizzle for about 3 minutes, until they smell delicious. Add your tomato sauce and the stock and cook for about 10 minutes, until the liquid has reduced by about one third. Transfer the mixture to a blender and blitz to form a smooth sauce. Set aside.

8. Remove the tatties and chorizo from the oven and tip them into a serving dish. Cover in your paprika-y tomato sauce. Serve with the delicious mayo laced (or not) with garlic, if you like.

Chicken Parmigiana

Fried chicken isn't just for buckets. Impress your mates with a fancy bit of plating that will leave you finger-licking, eyes-bulging, tongue-tantalising and whatever-other-body-part-wants-to-get-in-on-the-action-ing. With tomato sauce and all the right levels of cheese, this is chicken that will blow your socks off. Serve it with a simple salad and some cooked spaghetti.

Serves 4

The core
½ recipe quantity of **A Labour of Love** (see page 24)

For the chicken
5 tbsp **plain flour**
3 **eggs**, beaten
120–150g/4–5¼oz **panko breadcrumbs**
1 tsp **dried oregano**
1 tsp **smoked paprika**
2 **skinless, boneless chicken breasts**
about 100ml/scant ½ cup **vegetable oil**, for frying
salt and **black pepper**

For the topping
2 x 125g/4½oz balls of **mozzarella**, torn
50g/2oz **parmesan**, finely grated

*CHEF'S TIP
To stop the hot oil spitting in your direction, place one end of the chicken piece into the pan and lay it down away from you.

1. Preheat the oven to 200°C/180°C fan/400°F/Gas 6.

2. Pour all of your tomato sauce into a small oven dish and set aside.

3. Tip the flour into a small bowl, the eggs into another and the breadcrumbs into a third. Add the oregano and paprika to the bowl with the flour, season with salt and pepper and stir to mix. Set aside.

4. Slice each chicken breast horizontally through the middle to give you 4 similar-sized, thinner chicken pieces.

5. Now we are going to pane the chicken – this is the fancy term for breadcrumbing. One at a time, put the chicken slices into the flour mixture to completely coat. Then, dip each into the beaten egg, then finally into the breadcrumbs, making sure every part of each piece is covered. Set aside.

6. Pour the vegetable oil into a large frying pan so that it covers the base. Set the pan over a medium–high heat. When the oil is hot enough that the end of a piece of coated chicken sizzles as you dip, you're ready to fry.*TIP!

7. Shallow-fry your chicken pieces 2 at a time for about 5 minutes each side, until golden brown all over. (You don't need the chicken to cook through at this point because you're going to bake it, too.) Drain the browned pieces on kitchen paper and keep them warm while you fry the next batch.

8. Lay your crispy breasts on top of your luscious sauce and sprinkle over the mozzarella and parmesan. Bake for 20 minutes, until the cheesy topping is melted and golden. Get ya parm out the oven and serve up this beautiful, fancy dish to impress ya fam.

Aubergine Parmigiana

It's time to reclaim the aubergine emoji. We need to be sending 'aubergine emoji tonight?' to a response of joy at the thought of returning home to this mouthwatering aubergine parmigiana. This veggie dish will excite even the meatiest of meat eaters. These kind of aubergine pics are ALWAYS welcome. Serve it with a salad and some crunchy spuds (the ones on page 168).

Serves 4–6

The core
½ recipe quantity of **A Labour of Love** (see page 24)

For the aubergine parmigiana
4 **aubergines**
50ml/3½ tbsp **olive oil**, plus extra for greasing
2 tsp **dried oregano**
½ bunch of **basil**, leaves picked and torn
salt and **black pepper**

For the topping
2 x 125g/4½oz balls of **mozzarella or vegan alternative**, torn
50g/2oz **pecorino or vegan hard cheese**, finely grated

1. Preheat your oven to 200°C/180°C fan/400°F/Gas 6.

2. Chop the green tops off of ya aubs and slice them lengthways into slices about 5mm/¼ inch thick.

3. Get all your slices all in a row on some kitchen paper and sprinkle generously with salt. Leave for 10 minutes, to release the liquid. Blot the aubergines dry with kitchen paper (keep prodding to get rid of the moisture).

4. Grease 3 or 4 baking trays with a little oil and lay in the aubergine slices (they can overlap slightly, but if you don't have enough baking trays, do this in batches). Sprinkle with the 50ml/3½ tbsp of olive oil and the dried oregano, and season with salt and pepper. Bake for about 15–20 minutes, until a little crisp around the edges.

5. Start layering. Add a good 1–2 ladlefuls of tomato sauce into the base of a medium-sized ovenproof dish, then layer with the aubergines and a few pieces of torn basil.

6. Repeat the process of sauce, aubergine slices and basil until the dish is almost full (you're aiming for no fewer than 3 layers of aubergine, and don't forget to leave some space for the copious amounts of CHEESE). Finish with a thin layer of tomato sauce on top.

7. Sprinkle the mozzarella and hard cheese over the deliciousness, then get it in the oven to bake for 20–25 minutes, until golden and bubbling.

8. Once your parmigiana is ready to go, get it out of the oven and dig in. Most importantly, don't forget to slide into as many DMs as you fancy with your aubergine pic.

White Sauce

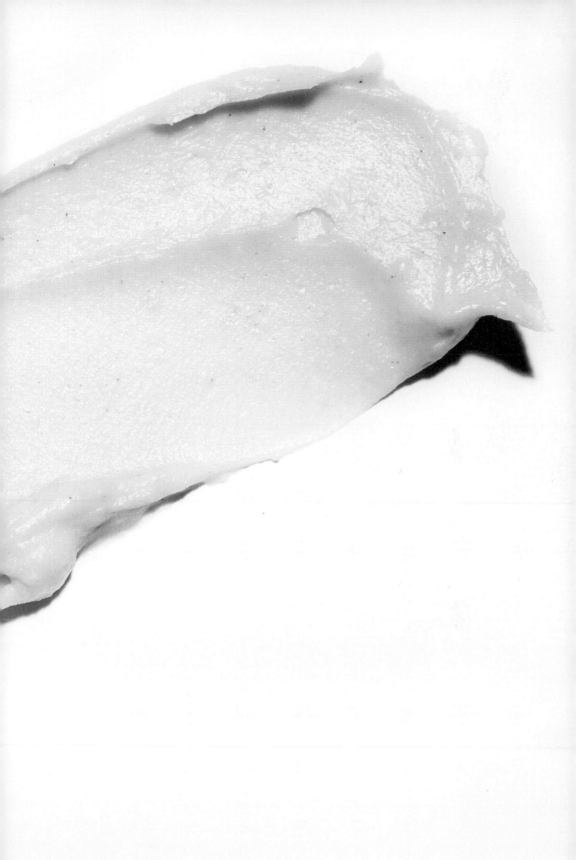

Béchamel

A béchamel is one of the mother sauces that you have to know when you go to catering college. There are a few ways to make a béchamel and they can result in various consistencies, but personally, I love a thick, gloopy white one. This is the kind that I think works best with the dishes in this chapter, but the book is all about adaptation, so if you prefer a thinner white sauce – just add a bit more milk.

Serves 4-6 (depending on how you use it)
- 500ml/2 cups **whole milk**
- 50g/2oz **butter**
- 70g/2½oz **plain flour**
- ½ tsp **salt**
- a pinch of **white pepper**
- ½ tsp **ground nutmeg**

For the fancy optional extras
- ½ **onion**, peeled
- 2 **cloves**
- 1 **bay leaf**

1. Pour the milk into a medium saucepan and place it over a medium heat for 7 minutes, until warmed through. Set aside. (If you want to get all fancy, darling, pierce ½ onion with 2 cloves and add this and a bay leaf to the milk while it warms. Remove just before step 4.)

2. Place a second, smallish saucepan over a low–medium heat. Add the butter and allow it to melt. Then, using a spatula or wooden spoon, gradually beat in the flour, about a tablespoon at a time, until you have a thick paste. You don't want the paste to start browning – if you're worried, just take the pan off the heat to slow things down a little as you add.

3. Once all the flour is in, cook, stirring, until you have a dough-like consistency and the paste is coming away from the sides of the pan.*TIP!

4. Little by little, add the warmed milk, making sure you allow the first addition to fully incorporate into the paste before adding more. Keep mixing to avoid lumps – switch to a whisk if you need to.

5. Once all the milk is in and you have a smooth, thick sauce, season with the salt, pepper and nutmeg. If you're not using the sauce straight away, transfer it to an airtight container (leave it to cool before you put the lid on).

*CHEF'S TIP
Stirring the flour and butter until it's thick is called 'cooking out' and it prevents that tacky, floury texture you can get sometimes with flour in sauces.

[STORAGE: FRIDGE **3 DAYS** / FREEZER **3 MONTHS**]

Cheese Sauce

It ends here. No more packet cheese sauces. It is literally so easy to make your own (it's just the béchamel with cheese in it) and I promise you'll be able to tell the difference. Forget the powdery texture and the 10,000 unknown ingredients that you just ignore on the packet. You know everything going into this baby, and it's all good stuff. Good stuff = good sauce.

Serves 4–6 (depending on how you use it)

- 500ml/2 cups **whole milk**
- 50g/2oz **butter**
- 70g/2½oz **plain flour**
- ½ tsp **salt**
- ½ tsp **ground nutmeg**
- 200g/7oz **your choice of cheese**, grated (I'd go for cheddar *and* double Gloucester, but a traditional Mornay sauce usually just has gruyère in there)

1. Pour the milk into a medium saucepan and place it over a medium heat for 7 minutes, until warmed through. Set aside.

2. Place a second, smallish saucepan over a low–medium heat. Add the butter and allow it to melt. Then, using a spatula or wooden spoon, gradually beat in the flour, about a tablespoon at a time, until you have a thick paste. You don't want the paste to start browning – if you're worried just take the pan off the heat to slow things down a little as you add.

3. Once all the flour is in, cook, stirring, until you have a dough-like consistency and the paste is coming away from the sides of the pan.

4. Little by little, add the warmed milk, making sure you allow the first addition to fully incorporate into the paste before adding more. Keep mixing to avoid lumps – switch to a whisk if you need to.

5. Once all the milk is in and you have a smooth, thick sauce, season with the salt and nutmeg.

6. Now, simply add your cheese and stir to melt in and combine for the perfect cheesy sauce! If you're not using the sauce straight away, transfer it to an airtight container (leave it to cool before you put the lid on).

[STORAGE: FRIDGE **3 DAYS** / FREEZER **3 MONTHS**]

Mac 'n' Cheese

Is there anything that says comfort more than a mac 'n' cheese? My relationship with mac 'n' cheese started off with a rocky patch – think bad experiences of packet pastas that ask you to add water... . No more. When you make your own sauce, the love changes completely. This is my go-to side dish at a restaurant, but, using this recipe, you can elevate mac 'n' cheese from a side dish to a staple dinner with a salad as a side.

Serves 4

The core
1 recipe quantity of **Béchamel** (see page 40)

For the mac 'n' cheese
90g/3oz **parmesan**, grated
100g/3½oz **extra-mature cheddar**, grated
150g/5¼oz **double Gloucester or red cheddar**, grated
1 tablespoon **salt**, plus extra to season
300g/10oz any shape of **dried macaroni**
1 x 125g/4½oz ball of **mozzarella**, torn

For the pine-nutty breadcrumb topping
100g/3½oz **breadcrumbs** (I like panko)
30g/1oz **pine nuts**, roughly chopped
black pepper

1. Preheat the oven to 200°C/180°C fan/400°F/Gas 6.

2. In a medium saucepan over a medium heat, warm up the béchamel, stirring to stop it catching on the bottom. Add the parmesan, cheddar and double Gloucester and stir to melt. Just keep this warm until you need it.

3. Three-quarters fill a large saucepan with cold water. Add the salt and bring the water to the boil over a high heat. Add the macaroni, stir to stop it sticking, then leave it to boil for 8 minutes, until al dente. (You don't want to cook it all the way as it will carry on cooking in the oven.)

4. While the pasta is on, make your topping. Combine the breadcrumbs and pine nuts in a bowl and season with salt and pepper. Set aside.

5. Drain the macaroni, then build this glorious comfort food. Throw half your pasta into a layer in a medium ovenproof dish. Mix in half your cheese sauce. Scatter the torn mozzarella on top. Add the remaining macaroni and remaining cheese sauce, then give the top layer another little mix.

6. Cover your big ol' mac 'n' cheese evenly with your breadcrumb topping, then bake for 25 minutes, until golden, crispy and oozing everywhere. Serve with a salad on the side, if you like. Everyone will DROOL.

Mrs Croque

Did you know *croque madame* means Mrs Bite? I feel a new nickname coming on. This is a shove-in-ya-face kinda dish, featuring a cheat's way to honey-glaze bought ham. As much as roasting your own ham saves money, sometimes you just cba for a snack. The fried egg, though, is a MUST.

Makes 1

The core
3 tbsp **Béchamel** (see page 40)

For the croque
2 thick slices of **crusty bread** (sourdough or a good ol' tiger loaf)
a little **butter**, softened, for spreading
100g/3½oz **your favourite cheese**, grated (I like a combo of mature cheddar, double Gloucester or red cheddar and parmesan)
a few slices of **ham** (I like to use the thicker-cut slices)
1 **egg**, plus 1 tbsp **vegetable oil** for frying it

For the cheat's honey glaze
juice of ½ **orange**
1 heaped tbsp **runny honey**
1 tbsp **Dijon mustard**

1. Set the oven to 'oven grill' and preheat to 200°C/180°C fan/400°F/Gas 6.

2. First, make the glaze. Stir all the glaze ingredients in a heatproof bowl and microwave on full power for about 30–60 seconds, until syrupy. (Use a small pan over a low–medium heat if you don't have a microwave.) Set aside.

3. Now for the croque. Butter each slice of your bread on both sides.

4. Heat a large frying pan over a medium heat. Add your slices of bread and fry on one side for about 2 minutes, until just coloured underneath. Remove from the heat and place the slices, golden sides up, on your work surface.

5. Layer up. Spread a spoonful of béchamel over the golden side of one slice of bread (you want it crispy inside the croque). Then, sprinkle one third of the grated cheese on top. Add the ham and drizzle over some cheat's glaze. Sprinkle over a further one third of the cheese.

6. Spread a spoonful of béchamel over the golden side of the second slice of bread, then flip it over and place it on top of the fillings, so that you have a full sandwich with a buttered, but uncooked top and bottom.

7. Heat the frying pan over a medium heat again and transfer this big beauty of a sandwich into the pan. Fry for 2 minutes, until the underside is golden, then carefully turn it over and fry the other side until golden, too.

8. Take the pan off the heat, and spread over the final spoonful of béchamel. Cover with the remaining cheese. Put your big croque on a baking tray and grill it for 5 minutes, or until the cheese is melted and golden.

9. Meanwhile, fry the egg to your liking in a little vegetable oil.

10. Put the croque on your plate and top with the egg. OH MY GOD, YES!

Bacon-y Garlic-y Potato-y

Okay. This is my official statement on achieving the perfect potato dish: bacon, garlic and potato are the ménage à trois that is out here changing lives. It's the modern-day throuple that's right every time. Unless you're veggie, that is – in which case, this dish is still a stand-out with just the garlic.

Serves 4

The core
1 recipe quantity of **Cheese Sauce** (see page 42)

For the gratin
4 large **potatoes**, peeled, and sliced into 5mm-thick (¼ inch) rounds
1 tsp **salt**, plus extra to season
200g/7oz **smoked bacon lardons**
3 **garlic cloves**, peeled and chopped
2 **rosemary sprigs**, leaves picked and roughly chopped
100g/3½oz **cheddar**, grated
black pepper

1. Preheat the oven to 200°C/180°C fan/400°F/Gas 6.

2. Tip the spuds into a large saucepan and just cover with water. Add the salt and place over a high heat. Bring to the boil, then cook for about 7 minutes, until tender.

3. Drain the potatoes in a colander, then suspend the colander in the potato pan and cover with a clean tea towel for about 5 minutes, until the potatoes have steamed off and dried out a bit.

4. While the spuds are boiling, add the lardons to a cold frying pan and place over a medium heat. Fry for about 6 minutes, until cooked through and golden. Remove the lardons from the pan and set aside on a plate lined with kitchen paper.

5. Tip one third of the spuds into a medium ovenproof dish, spreading them out in an even layer. Season with salt and pepper and sprinkle over one third each of the garlic, rosemary, lardons and cheese. Top with a good ladleful of cheese sauce (if it's been chilling in the fridge, you may need to spread it out a bit) and repeat twice more (potato, garlic etc, cheese, sauce), until the dish is full and you've finished with a final sprinkling of cheese. Bake for 30 minutes, until golden and a bit crispy on top. Dig in!

Beef Shin Lasagne

Lasagne is my Achilles' heel. I was vegetarian for two years... apart from three beef lasagne. My take on the classic incorporates my all-time favourite beef shin ragú that takes this pasta dish to the next level. This is the meal you whap out when your friends come over and they'll be posting it on the 'gram in disbelief. #foodporn

You're going to make a soffritto for this dish. Literally meaning to 'fry slowly', soffritto is a flavour base used in a lot of Italian cooking. It often consists of finely chopped onion, carrot and celery – but you can mix it up by adding pancetta, garlic and/or parsley, too. You can chop the veggies however you want as long as they are all fine and all the same size. I mean, you can use an electric chopper thing, you can use a mezzaluna (the double-handed rocking knife) or, if you're like me, spend some relaxation time chopping everything by hand using a super-sharp, but simple chopping knife. Once you nail it, you can pull out a soffritto for soups, casseroles, stews, ragú or anything saucy!

TURN OVER →

BEEF SHIN LASAGNE

Serves 6

The core
1 recipe quantity of **Béchamel** (see page 40)

For the lasagne
1kg/2¼lb **whole boned beef shin**, at room temperature
4 **onions**, peeled and finely chopped
4 **carrots**, peeled and finely chopped
1 head of **celery**, finely chopped
5 **garlic cloves**, peeled and finely chopped
6 tbsp **olive oil**
500ml/2 cups **good red wine or beef stock**
3 x 400g/14oz tins of **peeled plum tomatoes**
2 **bay leaves**
1 x 250g/9oz pack of **dried lasagne sheets**
1 x 125g/4½oz ball of **mozzarella**, torn
100g/3½oz **parmesan**, grated
½ bunch of **basil**, leaves picked and torn
a handful of **cherry tomatoes**, halved
salt and **black pepper**

1. Find the biggest pan you can — one that will eventually fit in all the beef shin and all the other ingredients. Heavily season the shin with salt and pepper and set aside. Combine the onions, carrots, celery and garlic in a bowl — this is your soffritto mixture.

2. Put your large pan over a high heat. Once it's hot — like smoking hot — add the shin and sear for about 5 minutes, turning frequently until browned on all sides. Remove from the pan and leave on a plate until later.

3. Reduce the heat under the pan to low–medium. Add half the olive oil and tip in your soffritto. Leave the veggies for 5–10 minutes, stirring occasionally, until they're evenly cooked and golden brown. Add the remaining olive oil and the seared beef shin (with any juices) to the pan. Give it all a good mix.

4. Add the red wine or stock to deglaze the pan (this is just a fancy way of saying throw in some liquid to get all that fried goodness stuck on the bottom of the pan back in your sauce). The liquid should make a huge TSIZZZZZZZZZ sound when it hits the heat — this is what you want!

5. Reduce the heat to low and add the tomatoes and bay leaves. Leave to simmer for about 4 hours, with the lid on, until the sauce is thick and the beef falls apart as you move it. (If it's not ready, leave it for another hour or two.) Once the beef is tender, turn the heat up, remove the lid and reduce the liquid so that you're left with a thick ragú.

6. Time to assemble! Preheat the oven to 190°C/170°C fan/375°F/Gas 5.

7. Bring a pan of salted water to the boil and get a large rectangular oven dish ready. (If your oven dish is oval, no worries — just trim the sheets to fit.)

8. Smother a thin layer of béchamel on the bottom of the dish.

9. Drop 2 or 3 pasta sheets into the water and boil for about 4 minutes, until flexible. Use 2 forks or a pair of tongs to remove them from the pan and layer them on top of the white sauce.

10. Add another 2 or 3 pasta sheets to the water and while they cook, top the pasta in the dish with another layer of white sauce, then with some meat sauce. Cover with the cooked pasta sheets. And repeat. The whole sequence, bottom up goes: white sauce, pasta, white sauce, meat sauce, pasta, white sauce, meat sauce, pasta, white sauce, meat sauce, pasta, white sauce, meat sauce, THEN (not pasta) — you end on white sauce.

11. Once you've completed your layers and ya lasagne dish is full to the brim, scatter over the mozzarella, parmesan and basil, and add the halved cherry tomatoes for extra boujee-ness.

12. Bake this glorious beast for 30–40 minutes — you're looking for a golden, cheesy top and bubbling corners. Ohhh! I'm hungry just thinking about it.

13. Carefully remove from the oven and serve with whatever you fancy. I personally like a crunchy salad with balsamic dressing. Maybe even a garlic bread if I'm needing extra comfort.

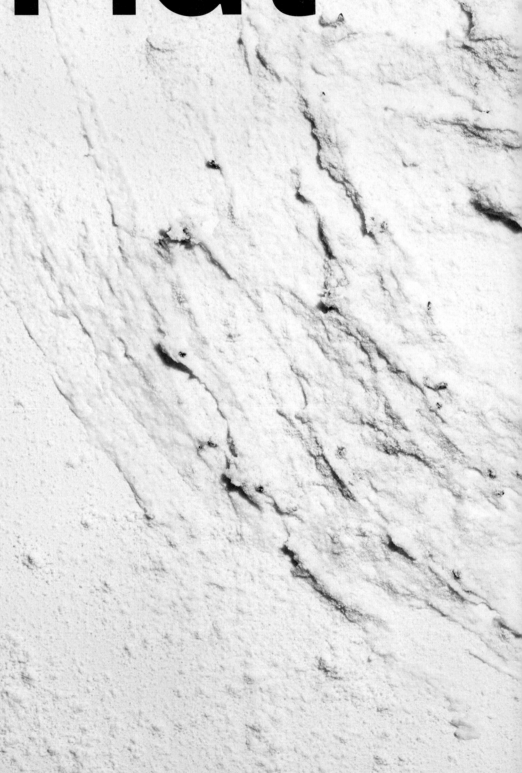

Flat

Bread

Easy Flat Breads

So much about 2020 made it a terrible year, but one great thing that came out of it for me was appreciating this flat-bread recipe. It's so, so simple. I'm one of those people (like my Mom) who heads to the shops almost every day because I've forgotten something on the big shop. During the height of lockdown, we weren't able to do that, but discovering how easy it was to make a flat bread meant that lunch was always sorted. Easy flat bread. Hummus. Dips. Perfection. But also a flat bread to use in so many ways.

Makes 4

> 250g/9oz **plain flour**, plus extra for dusting
> 250g/9oz **Greek yogurt** (**or** 125ml/½ cup warm water + 2 tbsp **vegetable oil**, if you're vegan)
> 1 tsp **onion seeds, poppy seeds or sesame seeds**
> 1 tsp **baking powder**
> **salt** and **black pepper**

1. This is literally so easy... in a bowl mix all the ingredients – flour, yogurt, seeds, baking powder and seasoning – into a dough. Knead for about 3 minutes, to a soft but not sticky ball. Cover with a clean tea towel and leave for 10 minutes to rest.

2. Cut the ball into 4 equal pieces and use a rolling pin to roll each one out to a thin round. You're aiming for them to be about 12cm/5 inches in diameter – but don't worry if they look rustic in shape. Set aside the rolled-flat flat breads on a lightly floured surface.

3. Place a large, dry frying pan over a high heat. Leave it to get hot, then throw in the first flat bread – no oil, no butter, nothing... just dry, hot heat.

4. Once bubbles start to form in the dough (about 30 seconds) and you've got a little bit of char on the underside, flip over the flat bread and cook the other side for about 30 seconds, to get a little bit of char there, too. Keep warm while you do the same with the remaining 3 flat breads. That's it, remove from the pan and serve (or cool and tightly wrap to store).

[STORAGE: AT ROOM TEMP **3 DAYS**]

Tikka Salmon

I'm a tikka kinda girl. I'm ashamed to say that as much as I try to pretend to be a food connoisseur, I order a Chicken Tikka Masala every single time from the curry house. This twist on a tikka brings it to a gorgeously fresh piece of salmon. Once wrapped up in your flat bread with lashings of mango chutney and cucumber salad, you'll never turn back.

Serves 4

The core
1 recipe quantity of **Easy Flat Breads** (4 flat breads; see page 56)

For the salmon
400g/14oz **boneless salmon fillet (skin on)**
3 tbsp **tandoori masala powder**
2 tbsp **Greek or coconut-milk yogurt**
juice of 1 **lemon**
1 tbsp **olive oil**
salt and **black pepper**

For the cucumber salad
juice of 1 **lime**
½ **cucumber**, sliced into ribbons *TIP!*
a small bunch of **coriander**, leaves picked and chopped
a small bunch of **mint**, leaves picked and chopped
a pinch of **flaky salt**

To serve
mango chutney
1 **red chilli**, sliced into rounds (optional; deseeded for less heat)
Bombay mix (optional)

> ***CHEF'S TIP***
> To get ribbons from a cucumber, simply use a speed peeler and slice off lengths in the same spot all the way through. Behold! A pile of long, thin cucumber ribbons.

1. Preheat the oven to 200°C/180°C fan/400°F/Gas 6. Line a baking tray with baking paper.

2. Pat the fish dry with kitchen paper, then place it on to the lined tray.

3. Mix all the remaining salmon ingredients in a bowl to create a marinade, then use this for smothering your salmon. You want a nice, thick layer.

4. Leave the salmon to marinate at room temperature for 10 minutes, then put the tray in the oven and bake the salmon for 20 minutes, until opaque and cooked through.

5. Meanwhile, make the cucumber salad. Mix together the lime juice, the cucumber ribbons and both the herbs. Season with the salt and set aside.

6. Heat a dry frying pan over a high heat until it's smoking hot. Place the flat breads in the pan and warm through. (Or reheat them in a microwave.) Set aside and keep them warm until you're ready to use.

7. Once the salmon is ready, smother the flat breads in mango chutney, top with gorgeous flakes of pink salmon and cover with your cucumber salad. I like to add an extra kick with some slices of chilli, and texture with extra-crunchy Bombay mix. That's it. Fold and eat.

Avo-bloomin-cado Brunch Wraps

I first discovered halloumi for brunch during my two years as a veggie and it's stuck around. It's the perfect light-but-still-filling hunger-appeaser for a late start to the day, and it leaves you feeling healthier than a bacon butty – even though, in reality, there probably isn't much difference in calorie count. Forget that – it's super-healthy. Tell yourself that instead.

Serves 2

The core
½ recipe quantity of **Easy Flat Breads** (2 flat breads; see page 56)

For the toppings
1 **avocado**, halved and stoned
juice of 1 **lime**
a pinch of **salt**
a good pinch of **black pepper**
a small bunch of **coriander**, leaves picked and chopped, plus extra to serve
½ **red chilli**, finely chopped (deseeded for less heat)
1 x 225g/8oz packet of **halloumi**, sliced into fingers
10 **cherry tomatoes**, halved

To serve
3 **breakfast radishes**, thinly sliced
a sprinkling of **pomegranate seeds**
olive oil, for drizzling

1. Scoop out the avocado flesh into a bowl. Add the lime juice, salt, pepper, coriander and chilli. Give it all a good smash with a fork, until you have a chunky guac-like consistency.

2. Heat a dry frying pan over a high heat. When it's hot, add the halloumi slices and fry, turning, for about 5 minutes, until golden brown all over.

3. Add the tomatoes and fry for about 3 minutes, until charred a little bit.

4. Remove everything from the frying pan and set aside on a plate. Carefully wipe the pan clean with kitchen paper, ready to warm your flat breads.

5. Get the dry frying pan over a high heat again until it's smoking hot. Place the flat breads in the pan and warm through. (Or reheat them in a microwave.) Now you're ready to load them with toppings.

6. Smother the flat breads equally with your avocado mixture and top with halloumi slices and those squishy tomatoes.

7. To serve, sprinkle over the radishes, pomegranate seeds and a few more coriander leaves, then drizzle with olive oil. Fold and dig in! A perfect brunch.

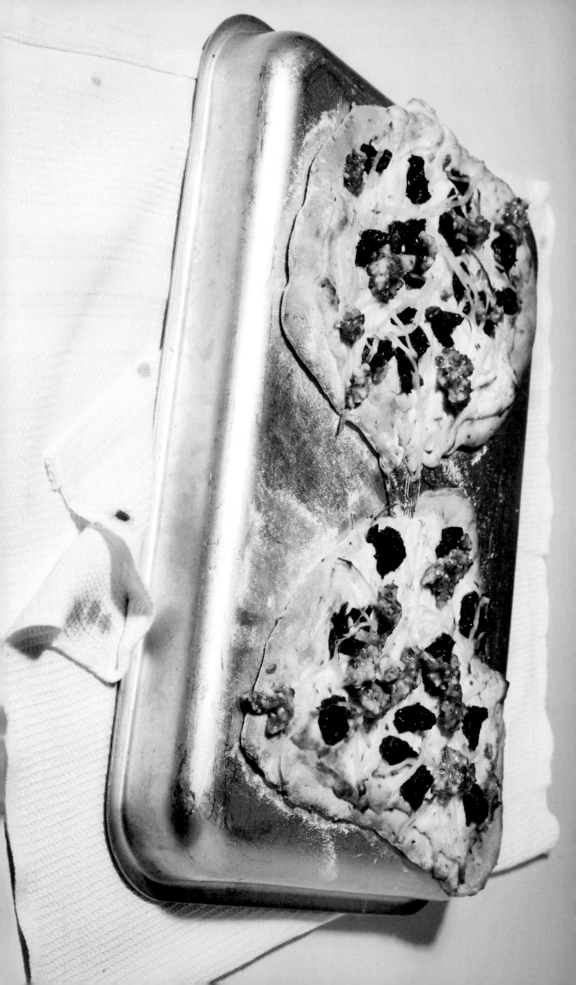

Potato-topped Pizza Spud Breads

The potato-and-bread combo should live for ever. I've taken that concept and made it a bit fancier with these (what I'm calling) 'spud-breads'. They're like a crisp sandwich, but posh. For this recipe, you'll need the flat-bread dough (not the actual flat breads), as it all goes into the oven together.

Makes 4

The core
1 recipe quantity of **Easy Flat Breads dough** (see page 56)

For the potato flat breads
3 **small-sized potatoes** (any kind), skin on
1 x 125–150g/4½–5¼oz round of **garlic-and-herb soft cheese**
10 **sundried tomatoes**, cut into little pieces
salt and **black pepper**

For the pesto
a bunch of **basil**, stems and all
½ **garlic clove**, peeled
50g/2oz **pine nuts**
about 3 tablespoons **olive oil**, plus extra for drizzling
50g/2oz **pecorino or parmesan**, grated

1. Preheat your oven to 220°C/200°C fan/425°F/Gas 7 and put a baking sheet or two in there to heat up (use upside-down baking trays, if you like).

2. Slice your spuds into wafer-thin slices. Then, slice them again into thin matchstick shapes – what I like to call 'baby fries'.

3. Arrange the baby fries on a microwave-safe plate in a thin layer and microwave them on full power for 3 minutes, until tender. (Or, blanch them in boiling water for 30–60 seconds, drain and leave to steam dry a little.)

4. Divide the flat bread dough into 4 equal pieces and roll each one to a thin round, about 12cm/5 inches in diameter (see page 56 for detail on the roll).

5. Divide the cheese round into 4 equal portions and spread 1 portion on each flat bread. Sprinkle the sundried tomato pieces equally over each.

6. Portion out the baby fries equally between the flat breads and drizzle with olive oil. Season with salt and pepper.

7. Carefully remove the baking sheets, or upside-down baking trays, from the oven and shimmy the flat breads on top. Put them in to bake for 15–20 minutes, until they are golden and crispy and the cheese has melted.

8. While the flat breads are baking, blitz up a pesto: put all the pesto ingredients into a pestle and mortar and crush; or whiz in a blender.

9. Once the flat breads are ready, drizzle over the pesto. You're good to go.

Slow-roasted Harissa Lamb Shoulder

These beautiful harissa spices give me flashbacks to a Moroccan holiday with my friends Jackie and Alex, although I can safely say the all-inclusive buffet of mostly chips and pasta didn't inspire this recipe. A slow-roasted number, it will turn even hardened lamb-haters – the meat just tears apart. Put in the effort with the prep, serve it up for dinner and spend half the night convincing your friends you didn't buy it ready-to-cook. Take the glory.

Serves 4–6

The core
2 recipe quantities of **Easy Flat Breads** (8 flat breads; see page 56)

For the lamb
2 tbsp **rose harissa paste**
3 tbsp **ras el hanout**
zest and juice of 1 **lemon**
5 **garlic cloves**, peeled
1 tbsp **light brown soft sugar**
6 **thyme sprigs**, leaves picked
6 **rosemary sprigs**, leaves picked
2 tbsp **almond butter**
2 tbsp **olive oil**
1.4–1.5kg/3–3¼lb **lamb shoulder on the bone**

For the couscous
200g/7oz **couscous**
seeds of 1 **pomegranate**
a small bunch of **mint**, leaves picked and chopped
a small bunch of **flat-leaf parsley**, leaves picked and chopped
5–6 **black or green olives**, pitted and sliced
1 tbsp **dried oregano**
juice of 1 **lemon**
salt and **black pepper**

1. Start this the night before you want to cook. Place all of the lamb ingredients apart from the meat itself into a blender and blitz to a smooth paste to make a marinade.

2. With a knife, make some little incisions into the lamb shoulder to help the marinade get right into the meat. Rub and massage the marinade into the shoulder like it's date night, until it's completely covered.

3. Transfer the lamb to a roasting tin, cover with foil and place it in the fridge overnight (or for a minimum of 6 hours).

4. Put the couscous into a container big enough to allow it to double in size and pour in 400ml/about 1½ cups of cold water. Cover the bowl and transfer it to the fridge. Leave this overnight, too.

5. Remove the meat from the fridge 30 minutes before you intend to start cooking so that it can come up to room temperature, and preheat the oven to 190°C/170°C fan/375°F/Gas 5.

6. When you're ready to cook, roast the lamb, still covered with the foil, for 4 hours, until it is charred a little on the outside and the meat is tender and pulls apart.

7. Drain the couscous through a fine sieve, so you don't lose any of it. Mix all of the other couscous ingredients into it. Season with salt and pepper to taste and leave on the side to come up to room temperature.

8. Towards the end of the lamb cooking time, heat a dry frying pan over a high heat until it's smoking hot. Place the flat breads in the pan and warm through. (Or reheat them in a microwave.)

9. Either serve your massive hunk of delicious lamb in the tin as it comes, or transfer it to a wooden board and pour all of the sauce that is left in the bottom of the roasting tin into a little jug.

10. Just let people dig and tear into this huge, sharing-lamb deliciousness, with the warmed flat breads, the couscous and the sauce served alongside.

SEE HOW IT SHOULD LOOK →

Emulsi

ons

Mayo

An emulsion is when an oil and liquid come together in harmony – that might be in a vinaigrette or a butter, or in this case egg is getting jiggy with some oil to make a mayo. When you master making your own mayo, the world is your oyster. Just think of all the things you could be adding to it for the ultimate fresh-at-home mayonnaise? Chilli? Garlic? Truffle? Mustard? Bacon? Onion? I'm in mayo heaven.*TIP!

Makes 1 small jam jar
- 1 **egg yolk**
- 1 tsp **Dijon mustard**
- 2 tsp **white wine vinegar**
- a pinch of **salt**
- 175ml/¾ cup **vegetable oil**

1. Tip your egg yolk, mustard, vinegar and salt into a bowl. Pour the vegetable oil into a jug, or something else that you can easily pour from.

2. Whisk the yolk mixture until it is well combined and a little fluffy. (This will help stabilise your mayo, so that it combines – emulsifies – properly.)

3. Then, super-slowly start trickling in the oil, a little at a time and whisking the whole time. This is mega important – don't stop whisking!

4. If you think the oil isn't combining, stop pouring and just keep whisking, which may just revive the emulsion. If it doesn't – see below...*TIP!

5. Once half the oil is in and the emulsion is thickening, you can increase the quantity of your trickle and you don't have to be so delicate (but do keep whisking). Keep going until you've used all the oil and have a lovely, stiff mayonnaise.

6. I like to add 2 teaspoons of cold water at the end to loosen the mayo slightly and give it a whiter finish. Transfer to a squeaky-clean, airtight jar.

*CHEF'S TIP

To make flavoured mayo, just substitute or add as you wish. So, to make truffle mayo or chilli mayo, simply substitute 50ml/3½ tbsp of the veg oil for truffle or chilli oil. If you want herby mayo, finely chop a small bunch of your herbs and stir them through. Easy.

*CHEF'S TIP

If your mayo is thin or split, down tools! Keep the mixture but get a fresh bowl. Crack in 1 egg yolk and start whisking. Add 1 teaspoon of white wine vinegar, then little by little, add your failed mixture, whisking until it all comes together. Once the failed mayo is in, just carry on with the remaining oil. If this doesn't work, get the blender out and go for it.

[STORAGE: FRIDGE **3 DAYS**]

Hollandaise

Once mastered, making hollandaise is like riding a bike – you'll be sorted for life. Friends round for the weekend? Whap out your hollandaise for a hungover brunch and prepare to WOW.

Serves 4

200g/7oz **unsalted butter**
200ml/¾ cup plus 2 tbsp **white wine vinegar**
1 **garlic clove**, peeled
6 **black peppercorns**
2 **banana shallots**, peeled and chopped
2 **egg yolks**

1. First, clarify your butter. Melt the butter in something that is square or rectangular, so that you end up with a thin layer. (In the microwave is the easiest way to do this.) Place it in the fridge to harden – about 30 minutes.

2. Poke a hole almost in the corner of the set butter and drain out and discard the buttermilk (the liquid underneath the layer of solid fat). There you have it! A container of easy clarified butter. Set aside.

3. Put the vinegar, garlic, peppercorns and shallots into a small pan over a high heat. Bubble to reduce for about 5–10 minutes, until there's about 2 teaspoons of liquid left (keep an eye on it so that you don't lose it all). Strain the liquid through a sieve into a jug. This is your reduction.

4. Get a saucepan and a bowl – the bowl needs to fit on the pan so you can have a good depth of water in the pan without it touching the base of the bowl. Pour water into the pan and place it over a low–medium heat.

5. Pop your clarified butter back into the microwave for a few seconds to melt it (or melt it in a separate pan over a low heat).

6. Once the steam is rising from the water, you can start making your hollandaise. (Make sure you don't let the water get too hot at any point – you don't ever want it to be boiling as it'll make the mixture too hot, cooking the egg and scrambling the whole thing.)

7. Tip the egg yolks and reduction into the bowl and place this over the water. Whisk for 1 minute, until the mixture has thickened a bit.

8. Very slowly, drizzle in the melted, clarified butter, whisking continuously as you go, until you have a thickened, velvety texture. Once it's like this, remove the bowl from the heat and your hollandaise is ready to use!

9. If you need to use it in a few minutes rather than straight away, place cling film directly on the surface (this stops a skin forming) and leave it near the hob to keep warm. Don't put it actually on anything hot or it will scramble.

[STORAGE: NO STORAGE / **MAKE IT, USE IT**]

The Chicken Caesar

This is a 'tell-yourself-it's-a-salad-so-you-feel-good-but-it's-so-damn-tasty' dish. This is no flimsy salad. It's a full-blown meal. But because it is a 'salad', put it on Insta, tag #salad and let everyone know how good you are.

Serves 2

The core
3 tbsp **Mayo** (see page 70)

For the Caesar dressing
½ x 50g/2oz tin of **anchovies**, drained and finely minced
1 **garlic clove**, peeled and finely minced
80g/2¾oz **parmesan**, finely grated, plus extra shavings to serve
1 **lemon**, for squeezing
about 1 teaspoon **white wine vinegar**
salt and **black pepper**

For the croûtons (or use store-bought)
a few thick slices of stale **sourdough**
1 **garlic clove**, peeled and halved
olive oil, for drizzling
flaky salt, for sprinkling

For the salad
80g/2¾oz **smoked bacon lardons**
2 **skinless, boneless chicken breasts**, sliced in half horizontally
1 **romaine lettuce**

1. Make the dressing. Stir the mayo in a bowl with the anchovies, garlic and parmesan (or throw these ingredients into a small blender and whiz).

2. Squeeze in a little lemon juice and add the vinegar. Mix, taste and add more lemon juice, and salt, if you like. Crack in some black pepper. Set aside.

3. To make the croûtons, preheat the oven to 190°C/170°C fan/375°F/Gas 5. Rub the sourdough slices all over with the halved garlic clove, tear them into chunks and scatter the chunks on a baking tray. Drizzle over a little olive oil, sprinkle over flaky salt and bake for 15 minutes, until golden and crunchy.

4. For the salad, tip the bacon lardons into a cold frying pan over a medium–high heat. Fry for 5–10 minutes, until the fat renders out and you have crispy nuggets of salty brown bacon-y bits. YES! Scoop the nuggets out of the pan and leave to drain on kitchen paper. Leave the fat in the pan, on the heat.

5. Season your chicken pieces with salt and pepper and get them straight in that bacon-fatty pan. Fry for 5 minutes each side, or until cooked through. (Do this in batches, if necessary.) Set aside while we create our masterpiece.

6. Tear up your lettuce into a big ol' serving bowl. Toss in three-quarters of your croûtons and three-quarters of the bacon bits. Slice your chicken into strips and throw them in. Pour over your dressing and give everything a mix.

7. Sprinkle over the saved croûtons and bacon, then add some parmesan shavings and serve as a massive, delicious sharing salad.

Eggs Royale

Eggs royale – with the poached egg and hollandaise – is only for fancy hotels, right? I don't think so! Bring the five-star treatment to your own bed. I'm hungry just thinking about it. Delicious.

Serves 2

The core
1 recipe quantity of **Hollandaise** (see page 72; make it fresh)

For the royale
a splash of **white wine vinegar**
4 very fresh, chilled **eggs**
2 **English muffins**, sliced in half
a little **butter**, for buttering
8 slices of **smoked salmon**
a few **chives**, chopped, to garnish
zest of 1 **lemon** (keep the lemon for squeezing), to finish

1. Get a small-ish saucepan over a medium heat and add the splash of vinegar. (The vinegar doesn't make a difference to the flavour, unless there's too much, but it helps set the egg whites, like in a meringue.) Wait until bubbles are slowly forming on the bottom of the pan and gradually rising up. This is when you know the water's ready.

2. Crack the first egg into the pan of water (if it helps, crack your egg into a little bowl or cup so that you can pour it into the water). Leave the egg for a few seconds, then tease it off the bottom of the pan by moving the water with the spoon.

3. After about 3–4 minutes, scoop your egg up using a slotted spoon and just give it a little poke to see how cooked it is. I like my yolk runny and my white hard. Drain the egg on a piece of kitchen paper, set aside and keep warm, and repeat for the remaining eggs. Now you're ready.

4. Toast and butter the muffins and arrange them on 2 serving plates. Stack the smoked salmon slices equally on top, and add the poached eggs. Dowse in hollandaise and sprinkle with chives and lemon zest. Give that lemon a little squeeze over. Dig in. (Be right back – I'm off to make Eggs Royale.)

Loaded Potato Salad

If you nail a good potato salad with your own fresh mayo, you'll be tasting summer any time of the year. Let's free potato salad from just summer. Winter potato salad? Sorted. Autumn potato salad? Yes, please.

Serves 4

The core
1 recipe quantity of **Mayo** (flavoured, if you like; see tip, page 70)

For the salad
500g/1lb 2oz **baby potatoes**
1 tbsp **salt**, plus extra to season
1 **lemon**, halved
a few **mint sprigs**
3 **spring onions**, finely sliced into strips or rounds
a small bunch of chopped **chives**
black pepper

For the crispy bacon bits
100g/3½oz **bacon lardons**, chopped small

For the crispy shallots
6 **banana shallots**, peeled, and thinly sliced into rounds
3 tbsp **buttermilk (or** 3 tbsp **whole milk** mixed with 1 tsp **white wine vinegar**)
200ml/scant 1 cup **vegetable oil**
3 tbsp **cornflour**

1. Tip the whole potatoes into a saucepan and just cover with cold water. Add the salt, 1 lemon half and the mint. Place over a high heat, bring to the boil, then cook for 15–20 minutes, until tender. Drain in a colander, discarding the lemon and mint. Leave to cool slightly.

2. While the potatoes are cooling, make the crispy bacon bits. Add the lardons to a cold, dry frying pan over a medium–high heat. Cook for 5–10 minutes, until the fat renders out and you have crispy nuggets of salty brown bacon-y goodness. Scoop them out and set aside to drain on kitchen paper.

3. Make the crispy shallots. Place the shallot slices in a bowl with the buttermilk for at least 10 minutes. Meanwhile, pour the oil into a medium saucepan. Place over a medium–high heat and heat it until a cube of day-old bread dropped into the hot oil sizzles and turns golden within 60 seconds.

4. Tip the cornflour into a bowl. Drain the shallot slices and dredge them through the cornflour. Tap off any excess flour and fry them in the oil for about 30–60 seconds, until golden and crisp. Drain on kitchen paper.

5. Halve any potatoes that are too large for an easy mouthful. Then, tip all the potatoes into a bowl and add the spring onions, chives, mayo, half the bacon bits and a squeeze of juice from the remaining lemon half. Stir to combine and season to taste with salt and pepper.

6. Sprinkle over the crispy shallots and the remaining bacon bits. Serve at any occasion! (Mainly just in ya jammies, eating lunch, watching telly.)

Steak Béarnaise and Crunchy Roast Chips

Date night isn't date night without a steak. And we're not excluding any single people here, because I'm more than happy to enjoy a date night with me, myself and I. Whether you're treating your partner or yourself, this steak béarnaise and my ultimate favourite potatoes will tick all the right boxes. A béarnaise is a tarragon-infused hollandaise, so we'll just use that core and adapt it slightly to make a delicious sauce for your steak. I'm serving it all with my signature crunchy roast chips – the easier method for the best 'CROUNCH'. And yeah, I spell it with an O in there to just make it all a bit crOunchier!

TURN OVER →

Serves 2

The core
1 recipe quantity of **Hollandaise** (see page 72; make it fresh)

For the roast chips
4 tbsp **vegetable oil**, plus extra for massaging the steaks
4 **maris piper potatoes**, peeled, and cut into thick chips/fries
1 tbsp **salt**, for the cooking water, plus extra to season
garlic salt, for sprinkling
3 **rosemary sprigs**, leaves picked

For the steak béarnaise
2 x 250g/9oz **rump**, **sirloin**, **ribeye or fillet steaks** (whichever you prefer)
a bunch of **tarragon**, leaves picked and chopped
a good knob of **butter**
1 **garlic clove**, peeled and smashed
a few **rosemary or thyme sprigs**
black pepper
your favourite **vegetable side or salad**, to serve

> ***CHEF'S TIP**
>
> To test if your steak is done, make an OK sign with the tips of your thumb and index finger and then turn it so your palm is facing you. Now, using your other hand, poke the thick bottom bit of your thumb and feel how soft and spongy it is. Now poke your steak – if it feels the same, it's rare. Now move your middle finger to your thumb and poke your hand again. It should feel tighter, like a medium–rare steak. Your thumb and ring finger is a medium steak and the little finger is well done.

1. Preheat the oven to 220°C/200°C fan/425°F/Gas 7. Sprinkle a baking tray with the vegetable oil for the roast chips and place it into the oven to heat up at the same time. Remove the steaks from the fridge and give them 30 minutes or so to come up to room temperature.

2. Make the chips. Tip the chipped potatoes into a saucepan and just cover with cold water. Add the salt and place over a high heat. Bring to the boil, then cook for about 7 minutes, until tender but not falling apart.

3. Drain the potatoes in a colander, then suspend the colander in the potato pan and cover with a clean tea towel for about 10 minutes, until the potatoes have steamed off and dried out a bit. (This makes them fluffier on the outside, meaning they'll get crispier.)

4. Carefully remove the tray from the oven and tip the chips into it, giving them one little mix so that they get coated in the hot oil. Sprinkle with garlic salt. Return the tray to the oven and roast the chips for 30–50 minutes, until crispy, golden and looking delish!

5. While the chips are in the oven, make the béarnaise sauce by simply adding the chopped tarragon to the fresh, warm hollandaise. Keep warm.

6. About 10 minutes or so before the potatoes are ready, cook the steaks. Heat a heavy-based frying pan or a griddle pan over the highest heat you can – you want the pan to be smoking hot. While it's coming up to temperature, pat the steaks dry with kitchen paper, then massage a little bit of oil into them all over and season well with salt and pepper.

7. When the pan is ready, get the steaks in it, laying them away from you so you don't burn your fingers.

8. How you like your steak cooked will determine how much time the steak spends in the pan. I would say, for an average-sized sirloin, very, very rare (or 'bleu' to be French about it) would be 1 minute each side. Then, you just add 30 seconds of cooking each side as you go up the steak scale. So, I like my steak medium-rare, which would be 2 minutes each side.

9. When the first side has done its time, flip the steaks and add the butter, garlic and some rosemary or thyme. Once the butter has melted, start basting the steaks with the lovely, herby buttery goodness.

10. After the total amount of time, check the steaks – you can do this with the thumb-and-finger trick.*TIP!

11. Remove the steaks from the pan and put them on a wire rack with a plate or baking sheet underneath. Pour over all the pan juices and leave them to rest for the same amount of time that you cooked them.

12. Remove the beautifully crunchy potatoes from the oven, sprinkle with rosemary leaves and divide the chips equally between 2 serving plates. Add a steak to each plate and pour over your incredible béarnaise sauce. Serve with veg or a salad.

Dre

sings

Vinaigrette Dressing

Once you realise how easy it is to make your own dressing, you'll never buy a bottle of it again. It's all about the ratios: two parts vinegar to nine parts oil. Once that ratio is right, go wild: add dried herbs, fresh herbs, finely chopped shallots; use different vinegars, different oils. Oh, you could use some of the confit garlic oil (see page 138) here, too – just keep the ratios the same. Feel free to halve (or double) this recipe.

Makes 1 small jam jar

> 2 tbsp **red wine vinegar**
> 9 tbsp **olive oil** (just ordinary olive oil, not extra-virgin,
>   which can overpower the flavour)
> 1 tsp **Dijon mustard**
> a pinch of **flaky salt**
> a crack of **black pepper**

1. Place all the ingredients into a clean jam jar and get that lid on tight.

2. Here's the trick for a well-emulsified dressing: shake the living daylights out of it. Get those arms working and feel the BURN.

3. After a few minutes, your dressing will be beautifully emulsified and ready to go. (You can, of course, use a bowl and a whisk or even a bowl and a hand blender. Either will give you the same results in your dressing – just not so much in your biceps.)

[STORAGE: FRIDGE **5 DAYS** (SHAKE BEFORE USE)]

Cheese Dressing

For a dressing creamier than a vinaigrette, it's less about ratios and more about ensuring you get the perfect consistency. This recipe is on point, and you can customise it yourself with any soft cheese you fancy.

Makes 1 small jam jar

100g/3½oz **soft cheese**, such as feta, blue or goat's
a squeeze of **lemon**
a pinch of **flaky salt**
a crack of **black pepper**
about 100ml/scant ½ cup **olive oil** (or enough for a mayo consistency)

1. Put the cheese, lemon, salt and pepper in a mini-processor if you have one. Otherwise, put them in a small bowl and use a whisk. Blitz (or whisk) until broken down and getting smooth.

2. Trickle in the olive oil, mixing continuously as you go, until you're left with a creamy, thick dressing that's ready for anything.

[STORAGE: FRIDGE **3 DAYS**]

Halloumi, Sweet Potato and Red Onion Salad

Salads can be so much more than just a side. This one, for example, is a really hearty dinner. It's fresh and healthy, and the cheese and carbs make sure it fills you up, too. And it's mostly just thrown into an oven tray. EASY! When it comes to the leaves and so on, feel free to add any other bits you fancy – these are just my go-to.

Serves 4

The core
Lashings of **Vinaigrette Dressing** (see page 87)

For the roasting tin
1 x 225g/8oz packet of **halloumi**, cut into 1cm-thick (½ inch) slices
2 **sweet potatoes**, peeled, and cut into 1cm/½ inch cubes
1 **red onion**, peeled, and cut into sixths
2 tbsp **olive oil**
1 tsp **flaky salt**
1 tsp **dried oregano**
1 **red chilli**, deseeded and chopped
2 **garlic cloves**, peeled and chopped
juice of ½ **lemon**
black pepper

For the salad
a small bunch of **flat-leaf parsley**, leaves picked and chopped
¾ **iceberg lettuce**, leaves separated and torn
½ **cucumber**, sliced into ribbons (see tip, page 59)
a small handful of **cherry or baby plum tomatoes**, halved

1. Preheat the oven to 200°C/180°C fan/400°F/Gas 6.

2. Tip all the roasting ingredients into a roasting tin, season generously with black pepper, and toss together so that they are well combined. Roast for 30 minutes, until the cheese is slightly golden and the sweet potatoes are tender.

3. Meanwhile, tip the salad ingredients into a serving bowl and toss together.

4. Once the halloumi and sweet potato mixture is ready, transfer everything straight into the salad bowl and again TOSS away to combine. Slather on lashings of the dressing, then plate up and scoff!

The Breakfast Salad

Now, I love me some black pudding – it's criminally underrated in the UK and deserves so much more than just being on the side of a cabbie's breakfast. Did you know in France it's called *bourdin noir*? How much sexier does that sound? Half of my family hail from the slightly less exotic Black Country in the West Midlands – where black pudding was a staple alongside raw sausagemeat (don't ask). This breakfast salad definitely has no raw meat, but it does bring a lot of the (cooked) things you love about a full English to a salad. If you're not as much of a fan of black pudding as me and my Yam Yam family, feel free to swap it out for sausagemeat.

TURN OVER →

Serves 2

The core
Lashings of **Vinaigrette Dressing** (see page 87)

For the croûtons
200g/7oz stale **crusty bread** (like sourdough), torn into bite-sized chunks
1 **garlic clove**, peeled and grated
2 tbsp **olive oil**
1 tsp **flaky salt**

For the salad
2 **maris piper potatoes**, cut into 2cm/¾ inch chunks
1 tbsp **salt**, for the cooking water, plus extra to season
200ml/scant 1 cup **vegetable oil**
200g/7oz **smoked bacon lardons**
150g/5¼oz **black pudding**, skin removed and lightly crumbled
    (or, use sausagemeat, if you prefer)
1 x 90g/3oz bag of **mixed peppery salad leaves**
black pepper

For the poached eggs
splash of **white wine vinegar**
2 very fresh, chilled **large eggs**

---

*CHEF'S TIP

Using a cold pan for your lardons renders out the fat, and then the heat slowly cooks the meat – giving you crispier, more golden morsels of deliciousness.

1. Preheat your oven to 190°C/170°C fan/375°F/Gas 5.

2. Make the croûtons. Put the chunks of bread, along with the garlic, olive oil and salt in a baking tray. Give it a good mix and bake for 10–15 minutes, until golden and crunchy. Set aside.

3. Start the salad. Tip the potatoes into a saucepan and just cover with cold water. Add the salt and place over a high heat. Bring to the boil, then boil for 10 minutes, until tender.

4. Drain the potatoes in a colander, then suspend the colander in the potato pan and cover with a clean tea towel for about 10 minutes, until the potatoes have steamed off and dried out a bit.

5. Meanwhile, heat the oil in a large frying pan over a high heat. When the potatoes are ready, fry them in the oil for 5 minutes, until golden. Remove from the pan and set aside to drain on a plate lined with kitchen paper.

6. Tip the lardons into a large, cold, dry frying pan, then place over a medium–high heat for about 5–10 minutes, until crispy. *TIP!

7. Using a slotted spoon, remove the lardons from the pan on to a plate lined with kitchen paper. Keep the fat in the pan.

8. Place the pan back over a medium heat. Add the crumbled black pudding (or sausagemeat) and cook for 7–10 minutes, until cooked through and crispy on the outside. Transfer it to the plate with the bacon lardons.

9. Now, you can poach your eggs. Get a small-ish saucepan over a medium heat and add the vinegar. When bubbles are slowly forming on the bottom of the pan and gradually rising up, the water's ready.

10. Crack the first egg into the water (if it helps, crack your egg into a little bowl or cup so that you can pour it into the water). Leave the egg for a few seconds, then tease it off the pan bottom by moving the water with a spoon.

11. After about 3–4 minutes, scoop your egg up using a slotted spoon and just give it a little poke to see how cooked it is. I like my yolk runny and my white hard. Drain on a piece of kitchen paper, and repeat for the other egg.

12. To assemble the salad, mix the black pudding, lardons, crispy potatoes, croûtons and a tablespoon of the dressing together and season with salt and pepper. Divide the peppery leaves between 2 serving plates and drizzle with some of the dressing.

13. Pile on the meaty mixture, drizzle on more dressing and top with your perfectly poached eggs. Splosh over more dressing, if you like, and, voilá! The best brunch.

Lemon-roasted Potatoes with Feta Dressing

For anyone who's followed me for a while on socials, you'll know that I had a lot of fun trying out potato dishes in my TikTok series *Around the World in 80 Potatoes*. The stand-out dish for me was the Greek lemonates patates – which has opened a whole new world in which I add lemon to potatoes.

Serves 2–4

The core
Plenty of **Cheese Dressing** (see page 88) made with feta

For the tatties
6 tbsp **vegetable oil**
6 **maris piper potatoes**, skin on and sliced into 2cm-thick (¾ inch) rounds
1 tbsp **salt**, for the cooking water, plus extra to season
juice of 1 **lemon**
70ml/⅓ cup **chicken or vegetable stock**
2 tsp **dried oregano**
2 tsp **fine semolina** (don't worry if you don't have any)
2 **garlic cloves**, peeled and minced
black pepper

1. Preheat the oven to 200°C/180°C fan/400°F/Gas 6. Spoon the vegetabble oil into a baking tray large enough to fit the potato slices in a single layer and place this in the oven to get hot while the oven is heating up.

2. Place ya spuds into a pan and just cover with water. Add the salt and place over a high heat. Bring to the boil and boil for 15 minutes, until tender.

3. Drain the potatoes in a colander, then suspend the colander in the potato pan and cover with a clean tea towel for about 10 minutes, until the potatoes have steamed off and dried out a bit. Then, give the potatoes a toss in the colander so that they break down a little on the sides.

4. Remove the hot baking tray from the oven and tip in the spuds. Give them a stir to coat them in the oil, then roast for 30 minutes, until part-cooked.

5. In that time, mix the lemon juice, stock, oregano, semolina (if you have it) and garlic in a small bowl.

6. Take the spuds out of the oven and turn the oven up to 220°C/200°C fan/425°F/Gas 7.

7. Pour the lemony liquid over the potatoes and give them a mix, then return them to the oven for a further 30 minutes, until crispy and golden.

8. Season the potatoes with salt and pepper. Serve with your cheese dressing on the side for everyone to spoon over or dunk into as they wish.

Buffalo Buttermilk Chicken with Blue Cheese Dressing

Now I love food. All food. Every recipe in this book makes me very excited. But if I had to choose one thing to have for the rest of my life, it'd be buffalo buttermilk chicken with blue cheese dressing. It comes from my family's love of visiting a popular American restaurant (often on a Friday) and ordering only starters... and lots of them. This evolution of the classic hot wing and blue cheese dressing takes things up a notch (or two).

Serves 4

The core
Plenty of **Cheese Dressing** (see page 88) made with soft blue cheese

For the buffalo chicken
280ml/1 cup plus 2 tbsp **buttermilk** * TIP!
1 tbsp **smoked paprika**
1 tsp **cayenne pepper**
1 tsp **white pepper**
1 tsp **garlic powder**
1 tsp **dried thyme**
1 tsp **salt**, plus extra to season
2 tbsp **jalapeño brine** from a jar (optional)
8 **skin-on, boneless chicken thighs**
about 1 litre/4 cups **vegetable oil**, for frying

For the salad
2 **romaine lettuces**, sliced
4 **celery sticks**, sliced
2 **carrots**, peeled, and cut into matchsticks or grated
½ **red cabbage**, shredded
2 **corn-on-the-cobs**
1 tablespoon **salt**
2 **avocados**, halved, stoned and flesh sliced
1 tbsp **jarred jalapeños**, sliced if necessary (optional)
black pepper

For the hot-sauce coating
100ml/scant ½ cup **Frank's hot sauce** (personal fave), or any other buffalo sauce
50g/2oz **butter**

For the dry coating
200g/7oz **cornflour**
1 tbsp **smoked paprika**
1 tsp **salt**
a pinch of **white pepper**

1. In a medium bowl, mix together all the buffalo chicken ingredients, except the chicken itself and the vegetable oil, to make a marinade. Then, add the chicken thighs and turn until completely coated. Cover the bowl and refrigerate for at least 2 hours, but ideally overnight.

2. To prep your salad, in a large salad bowl, mix together the lettuce, celery, carrots and cabbage. Set aside.

3. Place the whole cobs into a saucepan and just cover with water. Add the salt and place over a high heat. Bring to the boil and boil for about 5–7 minutes, until the kernels are tender. Remove the cobs and pat dry.

4. One at a time, stand up each cob and run a sharp knife down it in sections to remove the kernels. Keep the knife near the middle, stem-y/core bit for each swipe, all the way around. Gather up the kernels and set aside (discard the cores).

5. Make the coating. Get the hot sauce in a small saucepan over a low heat. Add the butter, allow to melt and stir to combine. Keep warm.

6. Pour the vegetable oil into a deep frying pan until three-quarters full and place it over a medium–high heat. When the oil looks hot, test a little nugget of bread in there to see if it's ready – if the bread starts to bubble and colour within 60 seconds, it is (soggy bread = heat the oil a bit longer).

7. Combine the dry coating ingredients together in a bowl.

8. Get the chicken out of the fridge and, one by one, remove the thighs from the buttermilk marinade, coating each in the cornflour mixture, then carefully dropping it into the hot oil. You can probably fit about 3 or 4 thighs into the pan at a time, so do this in batches. The chicken may spit a bit – keep your arms covered and use kitchen tongs.

9. Cook each batch for about 6 minutes, until the chicken is golden, crispy and cooked through (check it by cutting a piece open). Remove each cooked batch from the pan and set aside to drain on a plate lined with kitchen paper while you fry the remainder. Coat all the cooked thighs in the buttery hot sauce, then quickly finish the salad.

10. Add the avocado, sweetcorn kernels, and jalapeños (if using) to the salad bowl. Toss well and lightly season with salt and pepper. Place the chicken thighs on top, along with drizzles of any spare sauce. Slather generously with the cheese dressing, then serve up any remaining dressing at the table. This is naughty but nice in every way.

SEE HOW IT SHOULD LOOK →

*CHEF'S TIP

If you can't find buttermilk in your local shop, use whole milk to make your own at home. For every 250ml/1 cup of milk, you need to add 1 tablespoon of white wine vinegar or lemon juice. Just mix and it'll curdle for you!

Batter
Up

Tempura Batter

Batter is so quick to rustle up, it's no wonder most food has been battered in its time. Battered fish. Battered veggies. Battered prawns. We can even throw a Mars bar in there. Go on. Treat yourself. Beer batter (on page 106) is great if you have a big, chunky bit of fish, but if you're looking for a thin, crispier batter, tempura should be your go-to. The best news? It's easy.

Serves 2–4 (depending on how you use it)
   100g/3½oz **plain flour**
   2 tbsp **cornflour**
   1 tsp **salt**
   ½ tsp **caster sugar**
   180ml/¾ cup plus 1 tsp very cold **sparkling water**

1. Mix all the dry ingredients together in a mixing bowl.

2. Using a fork, mix in the cold sparkling water until just combined – do not overmix.

3. Use immediately – don't hang around otherwise you'll end up with brown, discoloured batter that no one wants.

[STORAGE: NO STORAGE / **MAKE IT, USE IT**]

Beer Batter

This beer batter will coat fish perfectly every time and – in case you were worried – it's just as easy as the tempura. The result is slightly thicker, which means it gives a gorgeous crispy edge to big chunks of fish. You can't get better than proper crispy batter, can you?

Serves 2–4 (depending on how you use it)

85g/3oz **self-raising flour**
85g/3oz **cornflour**
a pinch of **bicarbonate of soda**
a pinch of **ground turmeric**
1 **egg white** (**or 3 tbsp chickpea water**, if you're vegan)
120ml/½ cup **lager or sparkling water**

1. Mix all the dry ingredients together in a mixing bowl.

2. In another bowl, whisk the egg white or chickpea water until frothy, then add your lager or sparkling water.

3. Pour the wet mixture into the dry, gently stirring together.

4. Mix until combined (a few lumps are fine). Super-easy, there's your delicious batter!

---

*CHEF'S TIP

When you deep- or shallow-fry something, always place one end in first (just the tip) and hold it in the oil for a couple of seconds before carefully laying the rest of it down and away from you. This helps stop any scalding-hot oil splashing back at you. In shallow-frying, it also helps prevent the food sticking to the bottom of the pan.

[STORAGE: NO STORAGE / **MAKE IT, USE IT**]

Crispy Prawn Tacos with Sweetcorn Salsa

These prawn tacos will become an every-night favourite when you realise how easy it is to make tempura prawns at home. So quick and simple! The bite of a crunchy, fresh prawn in an easy-yet-delicious mixture of sweetcorn salsa with avocado will make you want to keep eating more and more.

Serves 4

The core
1 recipe quantity of **Tempura Batter** (see page 104) with
    1 tsp **smoked paprika** mixed through

For the salsa
1 x 200g/7oz tin of **sweetcorn in water**, drained
1 **banana shallot**, peeled and sliced
a small bunch of **coriander**, leaves picked and chopped
2 **avocados**, halved, stoned and flesh chopped
2 tsp **white wine vinegar**
1 tsp **olive oil**
salt and **black pepper**

For the prawns
200g/7oz **shelled, raw king prawns** (or more if you want fuller tacos)
about 100ml/scant ½ cup **vegetable oil**, for frying

To serve
12 **mini tortillas**, warmed
mixed salad, **red onion salad** and **sliced chillies**
your choice of **hot sauce**
1 **lime**, cut into wedges

1. Make the salsa. In a bowl, mix together the sweetcorn, shallot, coriander, avocados, vinegar and olive oil, and season with salt and pepper. Set aside.

2. Slice the prawns in half lengthways down the curved back. Remove and discard the waste tube at this point, too.

3. Heat the vegetable oil in a small frying pan over a high heat until very hot (the oil should be about 1cm/½ inch deep – add more if 100ml/scant ½ cup isn't enough). To test the heat, drop in a bit of batter. If it immediately sizzles, we are ready to fry.

4. Dip the prawns into the batter (do this 2 or at most 3 at a time), then pop them straight into the frying pan, taking care not to let the hot oil splash you. Fry for about 15 seconds on each side, until cooked through, then remove from the pan and set aside to drain on a plate lined with kitchen paper. Season with salt, then repeat the process for the remaining prawns.

5. Plate up 3 tortillas per person, load each one with salsa, mixed salad, a bit of red onion and some chilli slices, as well as your gorgeous tempura prawns and a sprinkle of hot sauce. Serve with a lime wedge for squeezing over.

Tempura Cabbage Fritters and Soy Dip

I know what you're thinking... cabbage for brunch? But let's revolutionise how we see cabbage. These beautiful brunch fritters are hashbrown-y (minus the potato), crunchy and delicious, and the dip is truly sensational.

Makes 6 (serves 2)

The core
1 recipe quantity of **Tempura Batter** (see page 104)

For the fritters
½ **white cabbage**, thinly sliced
3 **spring onions**, thinly sliced, plus extra to serve
1 tbsp **mixed sesame seeds**, plus extra to serve
½ tsp **chilli flakes**
1 tsp **dark soy sauce**
a pinch of **salt**
a pinch of **black pepper**
about 100ml/scant ½ cup **vegetable oil**, for frying
2 **eggs (or** 2 dollops of **vegan cream cheese)**
a small bunch of **coriander**, leaves picked, to serve
1 **red chilli**, finely sliced, to garnish (optional)

For the dip
2 tbsp **tomato ketchup**
1 tbsp **dark soy sauce**
1 tbsp **runny honey (or agave or maple syrup**, if you're vegan)
1 tsp **sesame oil**

1. Tip the cabbage and spring onions into a bowl and sprinkle in the sesame seeds, chilli flakes, soy sauce, salt and pepper. Mix together and set aside.

2. Make the dip. Simply mix all the ingredients together, done... Delicious and simple, just like me.

3. Pour the tempura batter over the cabbage mixture, mixing well to coat.

4. Heat 1cm/½ inch depth of vegetable oil in a frying pan over a medium–high heat until hot (add more if 100ml/scant ½ cup isn't enough).

5. Use your hands to scoop out a portion of the cabbage mixture. Use a spatula to carefully lower the portion into the hot oil, flatten it into a fritter with the spatula, and fry for about 1 minute each side, until cooked through, crispy and golden. Set aside to drain on a plate lined with kitchen paper and repeat with the remaining mixture to make 6 fritters altogether.

6. Reduce the heat under the pan. Using the oil that's in there, fry the eggs (if using) to your liking.

7. To serve, stack 3 fritters on each plate, blob on a couple of spoonfuls of dip and top with an egg or vegan cream cheese. Sprinkle with coriander and chilli to look like you just spent like 18-quid on it at a brunch restaurant.

Potato Bhaji Butty

You'll know by now that potato can take many forms. This is a spicy potato burger that doesn't miss the meat, giving a fresh take on a veggie option.

Makes 4–6

The core
1 recipe quantity of **Tempura or Beer Batter** (see page 104 or 106)

For the butty
1 **maris piper potato**, peeled, and cut into 1cm-thick (½ inch) rounds
1 tbsp **salt**, for the cooking water, plus extra to season
1 **red onion**, peeled and sliced
2 **garlic cloves**, peeled and grated
a thumbtip-sized piece of **ginger root**, peeled and grated
1 tbsp **vegan butter**, melted
1 tsp **chilli flakes**
1 tsp **ground turmeric**
1 tsp **mild curry powder**
1 tbsp **plain flour**
3 tbsp **gram flour**
about 5 **coriander sprigs**, chopped (stems and all)
about 100ml/scant ½ cup **vegetable oil**, for frying

To serve
4–6 **bread buns**, split open and buttered
4–6 tbsp **coconut-milk yogurt**
4–6 tbsp **mango chutney**
a few handfuls of **mixed salad or** a few extra **coriander leaves**

1. Tip the potato into a saucepan and just cover with cold water. Add the salt and place over a high heat. Bring to the boil, then cook for 7–10 minutes, until tender. Drain and smash the spuds (they don't need to be smooth).

2. In a separate bowl, mix together the onion, garlic, ginger, butter, chilli flakes, turmeric, curry powder, both flours and coriander. Add the mixture to the bowl with the mashed potato. Season with salt, then add just enough water (like a sprinkle) to help bind it together.

3. Get your batter into a bowl. Divide your potato mixture into 4 equal pieces and shape each piece into a large but flat burger shape (you may manage 5 or 6 good-sized patties – who doesn't want a cheeky freebie?).

4. Heat 1cm/½ inch depth of oil in a frying pan over a medium–high heat until hot (add more if 100ml/scant ½ cup isn't enough).

5. One at a time, dip your burgers into the batter to fully coat. Get each one into the frying pan and cook for about 3–4 minutes on each side, until golden and crispy. (You can fry in batches of 2 or 3 at a time. Set aside the cooked burgers to drain on kitchen paper and keep them warm as you go.)

6. Slather the bottom half of each buttered bun with coconut yogurt, place a patty on top and add a spoonful of mango chutney and a little salad or coriander... 'cause of, well, health. Top with the bun lid. Eat.

The DIY Chippy Dinner

Is there anything more British than a chippy tea? It's the smell. The taste. There's nothing else quite like it. To have the whole family sat around, eating food out of paper on laps, with the waft of vinegar running through the house — top-notch British teatime. And when you nail cooking it at home from scratch, it'll become a weekly treat rather than just a monthly one-off.

I don't know about anyone else, but I LOVE a good bit of vinegar. I've said to sprinkle your dinner with it at the end, but I don't really mean that. I'd triple, quadruple, anything-uple the vinegar amounts and have my fish absolutely dripping. And then I'd drink the vinegar out of the cone. But maybe I'm weird. Definitely feel free to add as much (or as little) vinegar as you fancy.

TURN OVER →

THE DIY CHIPPY DINNER

Serves 2

The core
1 recipe quantity of **Beer Batter** (see page 106)

For the fish 'n' chips
2–4 **maris piper potatoes**, peeled (or more, if you like)
1 tsp **salt**, plus extra to season
about 1 litre/4 cups **vegetable oil**, for frying
2 x 140g/5oz **skinless, boneless fillets of sustainably sourced
    white fish** (such as cod, haddock, hake or pollock)

For the quick tartar sauce
3 tbsp **Mayo** (see page 70; or use shop-bought)
2 small **gherkins (or cornichons**, if ya fancy), finely chopped
1 tbsp **capers**, finely chopped
1 **banana shallot**, finely chopped (optional)
a small bunch of **dill**, finely chopped
zest and juice of ½ **lemon**, plus optional lemon wedges to serve
black pepper

For the pea salad
200g/7oz **frozen peas**
1 tbsp **butter**
½ tsp **malt vinegar**, plus extra to serve

*CHEF'S TIP
Make sure your chips are well-dried after boiling, to ensure that they go nice and crisp when fried. Nothing worse than soggy chips!

1. CHIPS, CHIPS FIRST! Get your spuds chopped into chunky, chunky chip shapes – all similar sizes. Get them into a saucepan and just cover them with cold water. Add the salt. Place the pan over a high heat and bring the water to the boil. Boil the potatoes for about 10 minutes, or until tender.

2. While the potatoes are boiling, make the tartar sauce. Combine all the ingredients in a bowl, adding lemon juice to taste. Season with salt and pepper. Transfer to a serving bowl, cover and set aside.

3. Drain the potatoes in a colander, then suspend the colander in the potato pan and cover with a clean tea towel for about 10 minutes, until the potatoes have steamed off and dried out. *TIP!

4. Meanwhile, pour the vegetable oil into a deep saucepan – it should come about three-quarters of the way up the sides (no more). Place the pan over a high heat and heat the oil to 170°C/325°F on a cooking thermometer (or, until the oil looks like it's moving and dancing, like you can see ribbons in it).

5. Start frying your chips. Aim for 3 batches so as not to overfill the pan. Fry each batch for about 4 minutes, until the chips are crispy but not overly coloured (a light yellow – we're going to fry again later). Set aside each batch to drain on a plate lined with kitchen paper while you fry the next.

6. When all the chips have been fried once, turn up the heat of your oil so that it reaches about 180–190°C/350–375°F. It will take about 4 minutes – if you don't have a thermometer, test just one chip first.

7. Add those already-fried chips back to the hot oil, in batches again, for about 3–4 minutes, until they get extra-golden. Set aside to drain on kitchen paper again, seasoning them with salt. Keep warm.

8. Now it's time to batter your fish. One at a time, pat the fillets dry, then dredge them through your beer batter, making sure every bit is covered. (You want to do the whole process – batter and fry – one fillet at a time.)

9. Carefully dangle a little bit of your first fish fillet into the hot oil – ever-so-slightly – to check things are hot enough to go. The oil should start sizzling from just the little dip of the tip.

10. Carefully lay the rest of your fish into the hot oil, frying for 4–5 minutes, until cooked through with a beautiful, crispy batter on the outside. You may have to turn the fish halfway through cooking to make sure it's crispy the whole way round. Remove it from the oil and set aside to drain on a plate lined with kitchen paper. Repeat for the other portion of fish.

11. While the fish is frying, bring a small saucepan of water to the boil. Drop your peas into that boiling water for 30 seconds, then drain and place them straight into a food processor or blender. Add the butter and vinegar and season with black pepper. Then, just pulse until some peas are smooth and some are crushed. Set aside to keep warm.

12. Let's GO! I pile up my plate with the chips, sprinkling with plenty of salt and vinegar, and have the massive, crispy beer-battered fish on top. Serve with the tartar sauce and peas, and lemon wedges, too, if you like. Yum.

Savoury Pastry

Shortcrust Pastry

Now it's gotta be said. If a chef says they never use shop-bought pastry, they're probably lying. Puff takes days to make if you want it as good as the packet stuff, and filo is near-on impossible to make at home. Shortcrust, though, is super-easy and once you know how to make it, you'll be whipping it out on the reg. This makes enough for 1 large pie (lid and base) and 1 tart (base only) or three big tarts (just a base). Freeze what you're not using – then it's even easier to show off your pies whenever the mood takes you.

Makes 1 large pie (lid and base) and 1 tart (base only); or 3 tarts (base only)
- 500g/1lb 2oz **plain flour**
- 250g/9oz **butter**, cubed and chilled
- a pinch of **salt**
- 2 **eggs**, beaten then chilled
- about 3–4 tbsp **ice-cold water**

1. Using your hands, a food processor or a stand mixer, combine the flour, butter and salt. Either: with your hands, rub the ingredients between your thumbs and fingertips; in a food processor, use the pulse function; or in a stand mixer, use the paddle attachment and add the butter a few cubes at a time. Whatever the method, keep going until you have a breadcrumb texture.

2. If you're working by hand, make a well in the centre of the flour mixture, add the eggs, then the ice-cold water as necessary, and work quickly to incorporate. If you're using a food processor or stand mixer, add the eggs, pulse or mix, then add the water a little at a time. Once the dough starts to clump, tip it out and bring it together briefly by hand. You want just enough liquid so that the dough binds – don't overwork it, otherwise the pastry will be elastic, rather than crisp.

3. Divide the dough into 3 equal pieces and form each into a ball. Press the balls with the palm of your hand to turn each into a fairly flat, but fat disc (this will just help with rolling when you come to use the pastry). Wrap the pastry discs tightly in cling film and leave them in the fridge to rest for at least 30 minutes before using, or before freezing.

*CHEF'S TIP

Most tart recipes call for 'blind baking' the pastry case. This means giving it an initial bake without any filling to prevent a soggy bottom. To do this, line it with a large piece of scrunched-up baking paper and pour in plenty of baking beans or dried beans to keep the pastry weighed down so that it doesn't shrink too much. If you use dried beans, you can keep them to use again for blind baking – but don't try to eat them!

[STORAGE: FREEZER **3 MONTHS** (DEFROST FOR 4 HOURS OR OVERNIGHT IN THE FRIDGE BEFORE USING)]

Cheese and Onion Pie

This is the one recipe that I can't take full credit for. My friend KT, the token veggie in the friendship group since we were kids, once made this for me for dinner. My first instinct was... a cheese and onion pie? Bit basic, I'll probably miss the meat and I'll have to nod and smile as I pretend to really like it. But honestly, it was a game-changer. I've tweaked it a bit along the way and now it's yours for a weekly dinner.

TURN OVER →

→ CHEESE AND ONION PIE

Serves 2–4

The core
⅔ recipe quantity of **Shortcrust Pastry** (see page 120)

For the pie
½ recipe quantity of **Cheese Sauce** (see page 42)
a small knob of **butter**, for greasing
a little **plain flour**, for dusting
4 tbsp **olive oil**
4 **large onions**, peeled and sliced
½ bunch of **chives**, chopped
1 tbsp **Dijon mustard**
1 **egg**, beaten, for brushing
salt and **black pepper**

1. It you haven't already, make your half quantity of Cheese Sauce from page 42. Set this aside until you're ready to use it.

2. Grease a 20cm/8 inch springform or loose-bottomed cake tin with butter (you can use an oven dish, but a tin means you can remove this magnificent beast as a centrePIEce).

3. Lightly dust your work surface with flour. Break off two thirds of the pastry and roll it out to a disc about 33cm/13 inches in diameter and about 3mm/⅛ inch thick, keeping it as round as possible. The pastry disc needs to be large enough to overhang the sides of the tin. Re-wrap the remaining third of pastry and put it back in the fridge until later.

4. In whatever way seems easiest to you (I am a pick-it-up-and-hope-for-the-best kinda gal myself, but you could use a rolling pin to help you, if you prefer), carefully transfer the disc into the tin and gently let it sink into the hollow. Tear off a little bit of the pastry, roll it into a ball and use it to gently press the pastry disc into the corner around the base, and up the side to create a wall. Make sure there are no gaps or holes and that you have an overhang over the edge of the tin or dish. Pop this in the fridge to chill and rest while you make the filling.

5. Heat the olive oil in a large saucepan over a medium–high heat. When hot, add the onions and cook, stirring occasionally, for about 10–15 minutes, until they are just getting a tiny bit of colour. Season with salt and pepper.

6. Add the cheese sauce, chives and mustard, then remove the pan from the heat and transfer the filling to a bowl. Leave to cool slightly, then chill in the fridge for about 20–30 minutes.

7. Meanwhile, preheat the oven to 190°C/170°C fan/375°F/Gas 5. Roll out the remaining third of pastry on a floured surface to a disc about 24cm/9½ inches in diameter and about 3mm/⅛ inch thick, to form the pie lid.

8. Pour the chilled filling into the pastry case. Using a splash of water, dampen the rim of your pie and lift your pastry lid over the top.

9. Press the pastry edges together, then use a knife to trim off any excess. (You can use the trimmings to make decorations for the top, if you like – just stick them on with a little beaten egg.) Do a little crimpy, crimp between your finger and thumb or with a fork, to seal. Make 2 little slits in the top of the pie so the steam can escape and the filling doesn't ooze out.

10. Brush the whole thing with beaten egg, place on a baking sheet and bang the pie in the oven for 40 minutes, until you have crispy, golden goodness. Remove from the oven and leave to cool in the tin for 5 minutes before releasing and serving (or serve in the pie dish, if that's what you used).

Brekkie Quiche

Quiche is too often disregarded as just a dish your Nan pulls out at the family buffet. This one is glorious: all your favourite breakfast elements in a creamy, eggy base and held together in flaky pastry. Incredible.

Serves 4–6

The core
⅓ recipe quantity of **Shortcrust Pastry** (see page 120)

For the quiche
a little **butter**, for greasing
plain flour, for dusting
4 **pork sausages**, meat squeezed out and torn into small pieces
150g/5¼oz **closed-cup mushrooms**, sliced
180g/6oz **smoked bacon lardons**
100ml/scant ½ cup **whole milk**
100ml/scant ½ cup **double cream**
4 **large eggs**, lightly beaten
100g/3½oz **cheddar**, grated
a handful of **baby spinach leaves**
8–10 **baby plum tomatoes**, halved lengthways
salt and **black pepper**

1. Preheat the oven to 190°C/170°C fan/375°F/Gas 5. Grease a 23cm/9 inch loose-bottomed, fluted tart tin with a little butter.

2. Dust your work surface with flour. Roll out the pastry to a disc 30cm/ 12 inches in diameter and 3mm/⅛ inch thick. Transfer to the prepared tin, then tear off a little piece of the overhanging pastry, roll it into a ball and use it to press the disc into the corner and grooves. Trim around the edge.

3. Now we are going to blind bake it. First, using a fork, poke holes in rows all over the bottom of the pie crust, then line the pastry with a big piece of scrunched-up baking paper so that it covers the bottom and sides. Then, load up with baking beans or dried beans (see tip, page 120).

4. Bake the pastry case like this for 15 minutes, until just browning. Remove it from the oven and take out the baking paper and beans. Return the pastry case to the oven for about 7–10 minutes, until the bottom is slightly browned, too. Leave to cool while you make the filling (leave the oven on).

5. Heat a dry frying pan over a medium–high heat. Fry the sausagemeat pieces for about 5 minutes, until cooked through and golden. Remove from the pan and set aside. Tip the mushrooms and lardons into the pan and fry for 5–10 minutes, until cooked and browned.

6. In a large bowl, whisk together the milk, cream and eggs, and season with salt and pepper. Set aside a handful of the cheese and whisk the remainder in, too. Stir in the cooked sausagemeat, mushrooms, bacon and spinach.

7. Pour the filling into the pastry case, top with the halved tomatoes (cut sides up), sprinkle with the reserved cheese and bake for 40–50 minutes, until the filling is cooked with just a little wobble in the centre. Leave to rest for 10 minutes before serving warm (it's delicious cold, too).

Bombay Potato Pasties

What makes a better snack than pastry and Bombay potatoes? The answer... not much. These are perfect for a picnic hamper, or lunch, or as a get-home-late-and-line-the-stomach *need*. In fact, they're pretty much perfect for any occasion. Make sure you make a big batch of them so you can eat them whenever necessary – they'll freeze in an airtight container for up to 3 months. Just reheat them as you baked them in the recipe method.

TURN OVER →

→ BOMBAY POTATO PASTIES

Makes 4 or 5

The core
⅔ recipe quantity of **Shortcrust Pastry** (see page 120)

For the filling
3 **maris piper potatoes**, peeled, and cut into 2cm/¾ inch cubes
1 tbsp **salt**, for the cooking water, plus extra to season
1 tsp **ground turmeric**
1 tsp **black mustard seeds**
1 tsp **cumin seeds**
4 **dried curry leaves** (optional)
4 tbsp **vegetable oil**
½ **onion,** peeled and chopped
2 tsp **garam masala**
½ tsp **ground coriander**
1 **garlic clove**, peeled and crushed
a thumbtip-sized piece of **ginger root**, peeled and grated
½ **red chilli**, deseeded and chopped
½ **green chilli**, deseeded and chopped
1 tsp **tomato purée** mixed with 2 tbsp water
2 large handfuls of **baby spinach leaves**
a small bunch of **coriander**, leaves and stems roughly chopped
plain flour, for dusting
1 **egg**, beaten, for brushing

1. Place the potatoes in a large saucepan and just cover with cold water. Add the salt and turmeric. Place the pan over a high heat and bring the water to the boil, then cook the potatoes for about 7 minutes, until just tender. Drain in a colander, then suspend the colander in the potato pan and cover with a clean tea towel to steam off and dry out until needed.

2. Place a large, dry frying pan over a high heat and add the mustard seeds, cumin seeds and curry leaves (if using). Dry-fry for 45 seconds, until toasted and fragrant.

3. Add 2 tablespoons of the vegetable oil to the pan. Place over a medium heat, then, when hot, add the potatoes. Fry for about 3–4 minutes, turning once or twice, until the potatoes have a tiny bit of colour. Remove from the pan and set aside.

4. Add the remaining 2 tablespoons of oil to the pan and fry the onion for about 3–4 minutes, until soft but not coloured. Add the garam masala and ground coriander and fry for a further 2 minutes, until fragrant.

5. Add the garlic, ginger and both chillies and cook for 3 minutes, then add the diluted tomato purée. Stir to mix everything together. Add the potatoes back into the pan. Stir to combine, then leave to cook for 3 minutes.

6. Throw in your spinach and coriander leaves and stems, taste and give a last seasoning of salt. Remove from the heat and leave to cool.

7. Preheat the oven to 220°C/200°C fan/425°F/Gas 7. Line a baking tray with baking paper.

8. Dust your work surface with flour. Roll out your pastry into a large disc, about 3mm/⅛ inch thick. Start cutting out smaller discs, each the size of a side plate, re-rolling the trimmings as necessary, until you have 4 or 5 altogether.

9. Place about one quarter of the filling in the centre of each disc, making sure to leave enough space around the edge so that, in the next step, you can fold and seal properly.

10. Lightly brush the edge of each pastry disc with beaten egg. Fold one side of each disc over the filling to meet the opposite edge and create a parcel. Pinch the edges together in a cute shape or pattern to seal. It can look a bit like a seashell.

11. Place the parcels on to the lined baking tray and brush the tops with egg. Bake for 30–40 minutes, until golden and crispy. Eat warm or cold.

Stroganoff Pie

This is the kind of pi(e) that should be taught in maths lessons across the country (and it sure would've made me listen more). It's the pie that you pull together when your parents come to visit because you want to prove that you've got your life together and you're capable of fully adulting now. It's rich, it's decadent, it's fancy. Everything I'm not. I'm jealous of this pie.

TURN OVER →

→ STROGANOFF PIE

Serves 4–6

The core

⅔ recipe quantity **Shortcrust Pastry** (see page 120)

For the pie

50g/2oz **butter**, plus extra for greasing

2 tbsp **plain flour**, plus extra for dusting

400g/14oz **diced beef** *TIP!*

1 **onion**, peeled and sliced

2 **garlic cloves**, peeled and sliced

200g/7oz **chestnut or closed-cup mushrooms**, sliced

250ml/1 cup **beef stock**

2 tbsp **soured cream**

300ml/1¼ cups **double cream**

1 tbsp **Dijon mustard**

1 tbsp **smoked paprika**

5 **flat-leaf parsley sprigs**, leaves picked and chopped

5 **thyme sprigs**, leaves picked and chopped

juice of 1 **lemon**

1 **egg**, beaten, for brushing

salt and **black pepper**

***CHEF'S TIP**

To make this recipe veggie, in place of the beef and beef stock, use 600g/1⅓lb mixed mushrooms and 250ml/1 cup vegetable stock.

1. Preheat the oven to 190°C/170°C fan/375°F/Gas 5. Grease a 20cm/8 inch springform cake tin or a pie dish with a little butter.

2. Lightly dust your work surface with flour. Break off two thirds of the pastry and roll it out to a disc about 33cm/13 inches in diameter and 3mm/⅛ inch thick. The pastry disc needs to be large enough to overhang the sides of the tin or dish. Carefully transfer the disc to the tart tin or pie dish and let it sink into the hollow. Re-wrap the remaining third of pastry and put that back in the fridge until later.

3. Tear off a little piece of pastry, roll it into a ball and use it to gently press the pastry disc into the corner around the base, and up the side to create walls. Make sure there are no gaps or holes and that you have an overhang over the edge of the tin or dish. Transfer to the fridge to chill for 30 minutes.

4. Place a large saucepan over a high heat. Season your beef with salt and pepper and add it to the hot pan. Sear the beef, stirring so that it is browned on all sides, then remove it from the pan on to a plate.

5. Melt the butter in the same pan over a high heat. When hot, add the onion, garlic and mushrooms and fry for about 5–10 minutes, until there is some good colour on them all. Season well.

6. Add the flour (we're making a roux, like in the béchamel sauce on page 40) and stir until thick and clumpy. Little by little, pour in the beef stock, stirring continuously, until you have a smooth sauce with no flour lumps.

7. Add the soured cream, double cream, mustard, paprika, parsley and thyme, then tip in the seared beef. Stir well, then add a little of the lemon juice to season. Taste and adjust with more lemon juice, if needed. Remove the pie crust from the fridge and pour in the beefy deliciousness.

8. Lightly dust your work surface with flour and roll out the remaining pastry into a disc about 24cm/9 inches in diameter and 3mm/⅛ inch thick to form the pie lid.

9. Using a splash of water, just dampen the rim of your pie and lift your pastry lid over the top.

10. Press the pastry edges together, then use a knife to trim off any excess. (You can use the trimmings to make decorations for the top, if you like – just stick them on with a little beaten egg.) Do a little crimpy, crimp between your finger and thumb or with a fork, to seal. Make 2 little slits in the top of the pie so the steam can escape and the filling doesn't ooze out.

11. Brush the whole thing with beaten egg and place on a baking tray in the centre of the oven for 40 minutes, until you have golden pastry and a piping hot, creamy centre. If you're using a springform tin, leave the pie to cool for 5 minutes before attempting to release the beast and serving.

Confit

Garlic

How to Confit Garlic

Now, I love me some garlic! Disclaimer – the recipe I've given you is a realistic representation of how much an average household would use in a couple of weeks. The picture is a realistic representation of how much I would use. Confit garlic is such a winner – it's basically caramelised garlic that keeps for weeks in a jar. We've got some stand-out confit garlic recipes in this chapter, but don't let that limit you. You can pretty much use confit garlic as you would use normal garlic in any recipe.

Makes 1 small jar
2 **whole garlic bulbs**
about 200ml/scant 1 cup **olive oil**

1. Slice the bottom off each bulb of garlic just enough that you can see the garlic cloves inside, but no more. Remove the outer, papery skin of the garlic bulb to release the cloves, but leave the cloves themselves with their skins on. (I do this because it's easier to peel the cloves once they're cooked than it is to peel them raw.)

2. Place all the individual cloves into a small saucepan and cover well with the olive oil (use more if you need to – the cloves should be covered).

3. Place the pan over a low–medium heat and cook, keeping an eye on the temperature of the oil throughout – it shouldn't boil, but just gently plod along with the occasional movement in the garlic.

4. After 30–40 minutes, test to see if your garlic is ready: use a fork to lift out a clove and when it's cool enough to touch, give it a squeeze. If the garlic clove drops out from the skin easily and is soft and golden in colour, your garlic is ready. If it's not quite there yet, pop it back in for another 5–10 minutes and test again.

5. Remove the pan from the heat. Leave the oil to cool down completely, then carefully pour it, with all the cloves, into a clean glass jar. Seal with a tight-fitting lid. Use as needed – and that goes for the oil as well as the cloves. For the cloves, simply squeeze them out of the skin and away you go!

[STORAGE: FRIDGE **3 WEEKS**]

Greens Means Pasta

Eat this dish once and you'll just want to eat it more — think: cook on a Monday, then again on Tuesday... and again on Wednesday. Green food has a bad rep for being boring and un-tasty, but this pasta is here to turn that idea on its head. Garlic and pasta are quite literally a perfect pairing... and the confit element adds the richest edge to your fresh pesto. Best of all, the dish is so simple that it's ready in 20 if you follow my steps. We all need a roster of easy, simple dinners in our life, and this one will head to the top of the list.

TURN OVER →

→ GREENS MEANS PASTA

Serves 4

The core
3 **confit garlic cloves** (see page 138)
3–5 tbsp **confit garlic oil** (see page 138)

For the pasta and veggies
1 tbsp **salt**, for the cooking water, plus extra to season
300g/10oz **dried pasta** of choice
2 large handfuls of **frozen peas**
2 large handfuls of **chopped kale**
125g/4½oz **asparagus**, trimmed and chopped into 1cm/½ inch pieces *TIP!
2 **roasted red peppers from a jar**, drained and sliced
black pepper
parmesan shavings, to serve

For the pesto
50g/2oz **pine nuts**
zest and juice of ½ **lemon**
50g/2oz **parmesan**, finely grated
a large bunch of **basil**
a pinch of **flaky salt**

*CHEF'S TIP

When using asparagus, you can sometimes end up with a thick, stalk-y end, which is hard to chew and just not pleasant. Using both hands, bend the raw asparagus along the length of itself from bottom to tip, until you feel it naturally want to snap. Go ahead and break it at this point, to leave you only crunchy asparagus and less waste.

1. First, place a large saucepan of water over a high heat, add the 1 tablespoon of salt and bring to the boil.

2. Meanwhile, make the pesto. Put the confit garlic cloves, pine nuts, lemon zest and juice, 3 tablespoons of confit garlic oil and the parmesan into a food processor and blitz to a lumpy paste. (Alternatively, grind it by hand in a pestle and mortar.)

3. Add the basil and flaky salt and blend until smooth-ish and combined. If the pesto isn't coming together, trickle in a little more of the confit garlic oil to help. Set aside.

4. As soon as the water is boiling, add the pasta to the pan and boil until just undercooked (about 6–10 minutes, depending on the pasta). With a large mug, and taking care not to scald yourself, scoop out some pasta water for later. *TIP!

5. Add the peas, kale and asparagus to the water, bring back to the boil and boil for a further 2 minutes, until the pasta is cooked and the veggies are tender.

6. Drain the pasta and veggies in a colander and then tip them into a frying pan, along with the pesto, sliced peppers and reserved pasta water. Place over a low heat and mix to bring everything together. Serve up sprinkled with black pepper and scattered with parmesan shavings.

*CHEF'S TIP
When you're cooking pasta, PLEASE save a mugful of the pasta water just before draining it. The starch in the water is the perfect thickening agent for any sauce.

Ain't Mushroom for Lunch

DISCLAIMER! I am not responsible for the complaints of morning breath after digging down on this decadent, creamy, garlicky brunch option of mushroom heaven. Just FYI – I wouldn't choose this as a brunch following a first date, unless you want them out of the house quickly.

Serves 2

The core
2 tbsp **confit garlic oil** (see page 138)
6 **confit garlic cloves** (see page 138), 3 mushed, 3 whole

For the stack
4 slices of **bread** (I like seeded for this)
250g/9oz **chestnut mushrooms**, sliced
1 tbsp **butter**, softened
juice of ½ **lemon**
1 tbsp **crème fraîche**
1 tbsp **soured cream**
a small bunch of **flat-leaf parsley**, leaves picked and chopped
flaky salt and **black pepper**
20g/¾oz **parmesan**, finely grated, to serve

1. Using 1 tablespoon of the confit garlic oil altogether, drizzle both sides of each slice of bread in oil.

2. Using the 3 mushed cloves, spread confit garlic mush over one side of each slice of bread – use more or less, to taste... it's completely up to you how garlicky you want your breath to be.

3. Place a large, dry frying pan over a medium heat. When hot, add the bread slices and toast them for about 2–3 minutes each side, until golden brown on both. Remove from the pan on to a plate. (Do this in batches, if necessary.)

4. Increase the heat under the frying pan to high. Once it's smoking hot, throw in your sliced mushrooms, stir, cook for 30 seconds, then season with salt and pepper. Add the remaining tablespoon of confit garlic oil, reduce the heat to medium–high and continue mixing for a further 1 minute.

5. Add the butter and leave it to melt into the mushrooms, then add the 3 whole confit garlic cloves. Stir and cook for 5 minutes, until the mushrooms have a gorgeous golden-brown colour.

6. Add the lemon juice and stir to deglaze the pan, then add the crème fraîche, soured cream and parsley. Mix well to combine, then cook over a low heat for about 1 minute, until everything is hot, thick and creamy.

7. Place 2 slices of garlic toast on each serving plate. Top with copious amounts of creamy mushrooms and sprinkle with the grated parmesan to serve. Now this... this is a thing of great beauty.

Garlic-buttered Crispy Gnocchi

So classic, but so good! I've found that gnocchi are something you might order in a restaurant, but not necessarily make at home. There's something about making pasta that seems super-scary... but making gnocchi is so easy! Think of it as kinda one step beyond making mashed potato. Even successfully pronouncing the word *gnocchi* makes you feel sophisticated. It's like 'nyoh-kee'. Doesn't that sound fancy? And, you know what? These gnocchi are also gorgeous with the tomato sauce from the start of the book. Try both, then let me know which sauce is your favourite.

TURN OVER →

→ GARLIC-BUTTERED CRISPY GNOCCHI

Serves 2

The core
6 **confit garlic cloves** (see page 138), chopped

For the gnocchi
250g/9oz **red-skinned potatoes** (about 3 potatoes)
20g/¾oz **parmesan**, finely grated, plus extra to serve
a pinch of **ground nutmeg**
1 **large egg**
80g/2¾oz **'00' flour** (pasta flour), plus extra for dusting
1 tbsp **salt**, for the cooking water, plus extra to season
black pepper

For the sauce
50g/2oz **butter**
a large bunch of **sage**, leaves picked

1. Preheat your oven to 200°C/180°C fan/400°F/Gas 6.

2. Once the oven is hot, prick your potatoes with a fork, then bake them for 1 hour, until the flesh is cooked through and tender. Remove from the oven.

3. When the potatoes are hot enough to handle, cut them open and scoop out the flesh into a fine sieve. Press the potato through the sieve on to a clean surface. Weigh out 250g/9oz and discard (by which I mean eat) any that's remaining.

4. Place the 250g/9oz spud flesh into a mixing bowl (or you can do this on your work surface if you're feeling like a gnocchi pro) and, while it's still hot, mix through the parmesan and nutmeg and season with salt and pepper.

5. Make a well in the centre of the potato mixture and crack in the egg, then dust your hands with a little flour and use them to bring the potato and egg together. Once fully combined, add half the flour to start forming a dough. When that's mixed in, add the other half and knead to combine again. Stop kneading as soon as the dough is no longer sticky.

6. Take a quarter of the dough and cover the rest with a clean tea towel so it doesn't dry up. Using floured hands, roll the quarter of dough into a long sausage shape about 2cm/¾ inch thick and about 45cm/18 inches long.

7. Use a sharp knife to cut 2.5cm-long (1 inch) pillows of soft gnocchi. Transfer the cut pieces to a board dusted with flour and cover with a clean tea towel. Repeat the rolling and cutting with the next quarter of dough, and so on until you've used up all the dough.

8. Fill a deep saucepan with water (about three-quarters full) and add the 1 tablespoon of salt. Place the pan over a high heat and bring the water to the boil. Then, add the gnocchi to the pan, allowing them to sink to the bottom and bob around – when they float to the top (about 1–2 minutes), they're ready.

9. While all this is happening, make the sauce. Place a large frying pan (big enough to fit all the gnocchi) over a medium–high heat. Add the butter and leave it to melt. Add the chopped confit garlic cloves and the sage leaves.

10. As the cooked gnocchi come to the surface of the water, use a slotted spoon to transfer them straight into the sage-y, garlick-y, butter-y goodness.

11. Cook them in the pan until they're getting golden on both sides, giving the pan an occasional toss to prevent any gnocchi from burning. Transfer to serving bowls and sprinkle over some parmesan to serve.

Chilli Garlic Prawns and Polenta

Lockdown 2020 taught us that it's not always possible to get on a plane to enjoy a gorgeous holiday meal. No worries. Holiday in your kitchen with big, juicy garlic prawns. Whap on the summer playlist and grab the sunglasses.

Serves 4

The core
6 **confit garlic cloves** (see page 138), sliced
3 tbsp **confit garlic oil** (see page 138)

For the polenta
200ml/scant 1 cup **whole milk**, plus extra if needed
8 tbsp **polenta**
100g/3½oz **butter**
100g/3½oz **parmesan**, finely grated
2 large handfuls of **baby spinach leaves**
2 tbsp **sundried tomatoes** in oil, drained and roughly chopped
½ bunch of **flat-leaf parsley**, leaves picked and chopped
salt

For the prawns
200g/7oz **peeled, raw king prawns**
2 **red chillies**, deseeded and sliced
½ bunch of **flat-leaf parsley**, leaves picked and chopped
juice of 1 **lemon**
black pepper
a pinch of **flaky salt**

1. Make the polenta. Pour 500ml/2 cups of water into a large saucepan, add half the sliced confit garlic, along with the milk and polenta, and season with salt. Place over a medium heat and, using a spatula, stir to combine. Keep stirring (to prevent sticking) for about 30 minutes – bear with it, it's worth it! Add more water and milk if at any point the polenta looks like it's getting dry.

2. After 30 minutes, taste to check the consistency and seasoning. If you can still feel hard grains, cook for a further 5–10 minutes or so, and maybe add another splash of milk. Check again – you want it soft and smooth.

3. Add the butter, parmesan, spinach and sundried tomatoes and stir together to wilt the spinach, then remove the polenta pan from the heat, stir through the parsley and set aside to keep warm while you fry the prawns.

4. Place a large frying pan over a high heat and add the 3 tablespoons of confit garlic oil. When hot, throw in your prawns, the remaining garlic and the chillies. Season well with salt and pepper. Cook for about 3 minutes, flipping the prawns once or twice, until they are pink and cooked through.

5. Ladle a scoop of polenta on to each serving plate, top with a scoop of garlic prawns, then sprinkle with chopped parsley and lemon juice and serve.

Roast

Herb-roasted Chicken

I did an Instagram poll recently and it's official: chicken is your favourite roast of all time. When you try this compound butter method and work out the best mixture of garlicky herbs, you'll be wanting chicken even more.

Serves 4–6

1 x 1.25kg/2¾lb **free-range chicken**
2 **garlic cloves**, peeled and chopped, plus ½ **garlic bulb**, skin on
3 **rosemary sprigs**, leaves picked and chopped, stalks reserved
3 **thyme sprigs**, leaves picked and chopped, stalks reserved
200g/7oz **butter**, cubed and softened
zest and juice of 1 **lemon**, squeezed lemon carcass reserved
a few pinches of **flaky salt**, plus extra to season
a few pinches of **black pepper**, plus extra to season
1 **onion**, peeled and halved
1 **carrot**, peeled and halved
1 **leek**, trimmed and roughly chopped

For the gravy
500ml/2 cups **chicken stock**
2 tsp **cornflour** mixed with 2 tbsp water to form a slurry

1. Preheat the oven to 200°C/180°C fan/400°F/Gas 6. Bring the chicken out of the fridge for 15 minutes to come up to room temperature.

2. Tip the garlic cloves and both herbs into a bowl, add the butter and combine. Add the lemon zest and juice, salt and pepper and mush it all in.

3. Using a spoon, a spatula or your hand, separate the skin of the chicken from the flesh. Be careful not to tear the skin. Put the flavoured butter between the skin and the flesh of the bird. Place the squeezed lemon, half bulb of garlic and herb stalks into the bird's cavity.

4. Put the onion, carrot and leek into your roasting tin. Use kitchen paper to pat dry the whole chicken and season it well with salt and pepper.

5. Place the bird in the roasting tin, breast up, on top of the veggies, and roast according to the packaging instructions (usually 25 minutes per 450g/1lb, plus 25 minutes). To check that the chicken is cooked, poke a hole into the thickest part of the thigh – if the juices run clear, it's ready.

6. Remove the cooked chicken from the roasting tin on to a carving board and leave it, uncovered, to rest for at least 15 minutes.

7. Meanwhile, make the gravy. Put the roasting tin (with all the sticky bits in it) on the hob over a medium–high heat. Cook for 5–10 minutes, to get some colour on the veggies, then add the stock and cook for about 5–10 minutes, stirring with a wooden spoon to scrape up all the flavour stuck to the tin.

8. Add the cornflour slurry to the stock in the tin. Cook for a further 10 minutes, stirring so that no lumps form. When you're happy with the consistency, pass the gravy through a sieve into a jug. Carve, serve, enjoy.

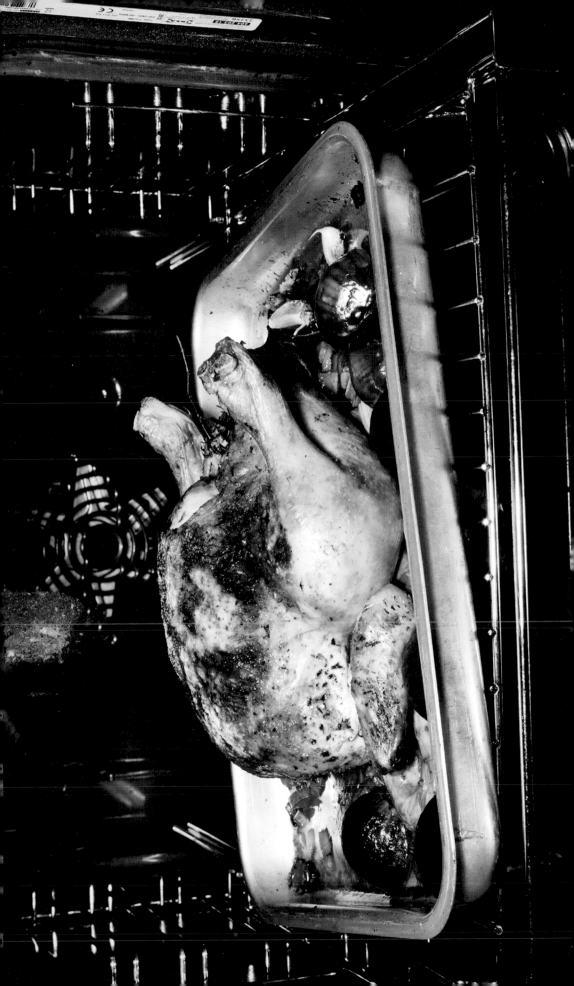

Apples 'n' Pears Pork

I love a pork roast, but part of me loves the next-day pork bap, apple sauce and stuffing even more. The addition of pear to this roast gives it something extra special, but don't feel guilty if you're more excited about a bap now.

Serves 4–6

2 **pears**, halved
2 **apples**, halved
2 **carrots**, roughly chopped
1 **onion**, peeled and roughly chopped
½ **garlic bulb**
2 **celery sticks**, roughly chopped
1kg/2¼lb **deboned pork belly**, skin scored (ask your butcher to do this)
flaky salt
about 4 tbsp **vegetable oil**
1 x 440ml/14½fl oz can of **cider**
200ml/scant 1 cup **apple juice**

For the sauce
1 tbsp **cornflour** mixed with 1 tbsp water to form a slurry
1 tbsp **unsalted butter**, chilled

1. Preheat the oven to 200°C/180°C fan/400°F/Gas 6.

2. Put the halved pears and apples in a deep roasting tin, along with the carrots, onion, garlic and celery.

3. Pat dry the skin of the pork belly and sprinkle a generous amount of flaky salt over the top, massaging it into the cuts. Set aside at room temperature for about 30 minutes, after which there should be some liquid on the skin. Pat dry again and pour over the vegetable oil. This is all helping to get that crispy, puffed crackling, 'cause what's the point of pork without crackling?

4. Place the pork belly into the tin, skin up, on top of the fruit and veggies.

5. Pour the cider and apple juice around (not over) the pork to cover the belly meat, but not the skin. If you need more liquid, use water or stock.

6. Roast the meat for 1½ hours, or until the skin is crackly and golden and the meat is tender. Remove the pork from the tin on to a carving board and leave it to rest for at least 30 minutes.

7. Meanwhile, strain the juice in the tin through a sieve into a medium saucepan. Remove the fruit from the sieve and set aside to serve, but squash down the veg to get all the flavour out. Place the pan over a high heat, bring the juices to the boil and let them bubble away until reduced by half (about 10 minutes).

8. Pour the cornflour slurry into the juices in the pan and cook for a couple of minutes, until thickened. Add the chilled butter and whisk together – this will emulsify into the sauce and make it extra glossy and luxurious.

9. I like to serve the pork belly whole to carve at the table with the fruit alongside, but you can carve it up beforehand to serve, if you prefer.

Smoke and Stout Beef

If there's one thing I've learnt from my Mom and stepdad Jim, it's how to appreciate a roast beef. I like my beef with a touch of pink and a thick, dark gravy – a decadent experience that requires a three-hour nap afterwards.

Serves 4–6

500g/1lb 2oz **beef topside** with a portion of **beef fat** (ask your butcher for it)
2 **onions**, peeled and halved
2 **carrots**, roughly chopped
2 **celery sticks**, roughly chopped
½ **garlic bulb**
3 **rosemary sprigs**
3 **thyme sprigs**

For the rub
1 tsp **smoked paprika**
1 tsp **light brown soft sugar**
1 tsp **garlic powder**
1 tsp **black pepper**
1 tbsp **flaky salt**

For the gravy
1 x 440ml/14½fl oz can of **stout** (**or** 440ml/1¾ cups **beef stock**)
500ml/2 cups **beef or chicken stock**
1 tbsp **cornflour** mixed with 1 tbsp water to form a slurry (optional)

1. Preheat the oven to 200°C/180°C fan/400°F/Gas 6. Remove the beef from the fridge for at least 30 minutes to come up to room temperature.

2. Make your rub: mix all the rub ingredients together... simples!

3. Put your veggies in a deep roasting tin and toss in the garlic and herbs.

4. Heat a large, heavy-based saucepan over a high heat. When smoking hot, add the beef fat and allow it to melt. Then, add the beef and sear it for 20 seconds on each 'side', so that it browns and will cook evenly.

5. Place the beef on top of the veggies in the tin and roast for 50 minutes, until medium–rare. Remove from the oven and pour out the pan juices into a bowl. Transfer the meat to a carving board and leave it to rest for about 50 minutes – this may seem a long time, but cooking time = resting time.

6. Put the roasting tin on the hob over a medium–high heat and cook for about 5–10 minutes, until the veggies are browned. Add back the pan juices with the stout (or stock) and deglaze the pan, scraping the bottom with a wooden spoon. Leave the liquid to bubble away for about 10–15 minutes, until reduced by half (keep an eye on it so that it doesn't reduce too much). Add the stock and bubble again until reduced by a third.

7. Strain the gravy through a sieve into a small saucepan, pushing down on the contents of the sieve to get all the flavour out. Place the pan over a medium heat and, if it's not thick enough, add the cornflour slurry to thicken to your preferred consistency. Now you're ready to carve and serve.

Red Onion Tarte Tatin

True story: I once cooked this for a party and had at least three people ask me for the recipe the next morning. I am 100% that friend who puts out a spread at a party, as well as the Cheeky Vimto and a sharer bag of crisps.

Serves 4–6

4–5 **red onions**, peeled and halved
3 tbsp **light brown soft sugar**
1 tbsp **balsamic vinegar**
50g/2oz **vegan spread**, plus 1 tbsp melted
1 x 320g/11oz sheet of **ready-rolled vegan puff pastry**
3 **thyme sprigs**, leaves picked
flaky salt and **black pepper**

1. Preheat the oven to 220°C/200°C fan/425°F/Gas 7.

2. Check that your onion halves fit neatly in a medium, oven-friendly frying pan. You want them to look like a little flower – one half in the centre, then the other halves around the outside. Adjust the number of onion halves for a snug fit. Remove the onions and get the pan on the hob over a medium heat.

3. Add the sugar to the pan and leave it to melt for about 4 minutes. Stir in the vinegar, then stir in the 50g/2oz of vegan spread.

4. Place the onions in the pan, cut sides down, in the flower arrangement. Reduce the heat a little and leave the onions for about 10 minutes, to get some colour – keep an eye on them and turn the heat down more if the sugar is getting too thick or burning. If it does burn, keep calm! Remove the onions from the pan, remake the caramel and put the onions back. Breathe.

5. Lay out the sheet of puff pastry and place a plate on top (find one a similar size to the frying pan). Use it as a guide to cut out a pastry circle.

6. Once the onions are nicely caramelised and you have a thick sauce on the base of the pan, remove the pan from the heat and place your pastry circle on top of the onions, tucking the edge down into the pan.

7. Brush the melted vegan spread over the pastry, then place the frying pan in the oven to bake the tart for about 15–20 minutes, or until the pastry has puffed up and is golden and crispy. Remove the pan from the oven and place it on a folded tea towel (to stop you burning your hand in the next step).

8. Grab a plate that is a bit bigger than the pan. Place the plate on top of the pan – you're going to flip your tart. Hold the plate in place with your dominant hand and hold the bottom of the pan (complete with the tea towel for protection) with your non-dominant hand. Confidently flip the pan, keeping your hands tightly on the pan and plate.

9. Lift the pan away from the plate and you should be left with a beautiful tart. Sometimes the onions can stick to the pan – just carefully remove them, placing them into the spare slots, and get any remaining sauce out. Sprinkle over the thyme leaves and season with flaky salt and black pepper.

A Good Pork Stuffing

Stuffing is one of those things that will always be great out of a packet. I spend my career encouraging people to cook from scratch, but packet stuffing... a winner. That said, making your own really is unbeatable – with the freshness and meatiness giving it the upper hand. Just remember to make excess so that you have enough for sandwiches the next day.

Serves 4–6

½ stale loaf of **any bread**
a little **vegetable oil**, for frying
2 **red onions**, peeled and finely chopped
1 **garlic clove**, peeled and chopped
400g/14oz **sausagemeat** (for a meat-free option use breadcrumbs made using the other half of the stale loaf)
3 **rosemary sprigs**, leaves picked and chopped
3 **thyme sprigs**, leaves picked and chopped
300ml/1¼ cups **chicken or vegetable stock**, warmed
salt and **black pepper**

1. If your bread isn't that stale, tear it up and put the chunks in the oven at 120°C/100°C fan/235°F/Gas ¾ for about 10–20 minutes, until dry. Blitz the bread (or chunks if you'd dried it out) until you have breadcrumbs.

2. Preheat the oven to 200°C/180°C fan/400°F/Gas 6.

3. Heat the vegetable oil in a frying pan over a medium heat. When hot, add the onions and fry for 1–2 minutes, then add the garlic and cook for 6 minutes, until everything is soft but not coloured.

4. Add the breadcrumbs and sausagemeat (or further breadcrumbs) and both herbs, then season heavily with salt and pepper. Give it all a good mix (I find using my hands is the best way) until combined. Pour over the stock.

5. Transfer the stuffing to a 450g/1lb loaf tin and bake it for 30 minutes, until cooked through and golden and crunchy.

Potatoes Boulangère

There are worse decisions to be making than which delicious potatoes will go with your roast dinner. I'd be tempted to go with all three in this chapter (yep, there are two more coming...). Boulangère are like dauphinoise, but with meaty stock instead of cream. I first tried them last year and they soon made their way towards the top of my potato list. Could I say all the way to the top? It'd be like choosing between my children.

Serves 4–6

50g/2oz **butter**
2 tbsp **olive oil**
5 **red-skinned or russet potatoes**, peeled, and sliced into 5mm/¼ inch rounds
2 **onions**, peeled, and sliced into 5mm/¼ inch rounds
1 **garlic clove**, peeled and chopped
1 **chicken or vegetable stock pot or cube**
200ml/scant 1 cup **boiling water**
salt and **black pepper**

1. Preheat the oven to 200°C/180°C fan/400°F/Gas 6.

2. Melt the butter with the oil in a large saucepan over a medium–high heat. Add the potatoes and onions and fry (in batches, if necessary), for about 10 minutes, until some pieces have browned slightly. Season with salt and pepper.

3. Add the garlic and then tip everything straight into a medium-sized, deep, round ovenproof dish (it needs to be about 7cm/3 inches deep).

4. Put the stock pot or cube into a jug and pour in the boiling water. Stir until dissolved, then pour the stock into the dish to just cover the potatoes.

5. Bake for 20–30 minutes, until the potatoes are tender, and they are browned and sticky on top.

← SEE HOW IT SHOULD LOOK (PAGE 164)

Apple Mash

Another potato classic and a method that will serve you long after you've finished making your way through this book. I really think I've cracked the perfect, smooth mashed potato. I love it – creamy and luscious. In this recipe, I've added an apple edge because I'm prone to covering everything in apple sauce. This makes it a perfect accompaniment to chicken or pork, or you could swap out the apple for a bit of mustard to go with your beef, or use vegan alternatives to eat with your tatin.

Serves 4–6

4 **maris piper potatoes**, peeled, and sliced into 1cm-thick (½ inch) rounds
1 **cooking apple**, peeled, cored, and cut into 2cm/¾ inch chunks
1 tbsp **salt**, for the cooking water
75g/2½oz **butter**, plus optional extra, melted, for brushing
50ml/3½ tbsp **whole milk or full-fat cream** (if you feel extra-naughty), warmed

1. Tip the potatoes and apple into a saucepan and just cover with cold water. Add the salt and place over a high heat. Bring to the simmer, then keep at a steady simmer (simmering, not boiling, for an even cook) for about 15 minutes, until the potatoes slide off when you poke them with the point of a knife. You're good to go!

2. Drain the potatoes and apple into a colander, suspend the colander in the cooking pan, cover with a clean tea towel and allow to steam-dry for about 10 minutes.

3. Add the butter (this helps to coat the potato particles as they mash, and keeps them fluffy), then begin to pass the potato and apple mixture through a sieve or potato ricer into a large bowl.

4. Add the warmed milk or cream to the bowl and stir until just combined. The less stirring you do, the less elasticated your mash will be.

5. Now, I like to go all out and get this into a piping bag and pipe the mash into a dish. It's optional whether or not you want to bake it to get a crusty top, but if you do: pipe it, brush over the top with melted butter, if you wish, and bake it in the oven for 10–15 minutes at 200°C/180°C fan/400°F/Gas 6.

← SEE HOW IT SHOULD LOOK (PAGE 164)

Roast Tatties

I make these potatoes over and over again – every weekend. This simple, yet effective recipe is the perfect way to get that CROUNCH. And, yes, I'm still talking about crOunchy potatoes. It's like your everyday crunchy, but with added ooooooo. Heavenly.

Serves 4–6

at least 6 **maris piper potatoes**, peeled
1 tbsp **salt**, for the cooking water
3½ tbsp **vegetable oil**
flaky salt

1. Cut your potatoes into quarters – so the pieces are nice and big and chunky! This will help give you fluffy, crispy edges.

2. Tip them into a large saucepan and just cover with cold water. Add the salt and place over a high heat. Bring to the boil, then cook for about 15 minutes, or until you can poke the potatoes with the tip of a knife and they fall off.

3. Drain the potatoes in a colander, then suspend the colander in the potato pan and cover with a clean tea towel for about 10–15 minutes, until the potatoes have steamed off and dried out a bit. *TIP!

4. While your potatoes are steam-drying, preheat the oven to 220°C/200°C fan/425°F/Gas 7. Pour the vegetable oil into a baking tray big enough to fit the potatoes in a single layer and place this in the oven to get hot while the oven is heating up.

5. Once the tatties have dried out, give them a shake in the colander so that the sides of the spuds get all broken and crumbly.

6. Carefully get the baking tray out of the oven and tip in the spuds. Give them a toss to get them coated in the oil, then return them to the oven to roast for 20 minutes. Give them another toss, then leave them in the oven for a further 20–30 minutes, until they are golden and crispy.

7. Remove from the oven and serve sprinkled with plenty of flaky salt. *TIP

> ***CHEF'S TIP**
>
> *Steam-drying parboiled potatoes – in a colander, set in the cooking pan and covered with a clean tea towel – keeps the steam locked in and gives the spuds a bit of time to dry out on the outside, resulting in a crispier exterior and fluffier interior in the finished roastie.*

> ***CHEF'S TIP**
>
> *If you fancy changing your roastie game, at the end of cooking, try adding some different flavours, such as a sprinkle of grated parmesan or some chopped rosemary and garlic. You could even drizzle over some truffle oil to make the spuds extra fancy.*

Yorkshire Puds

Controversial, but I'd be happy with a Yorkshire pud not just with beef, but with any roast dinner. I want to apologise to the great aunt sometimes known as Bessie, as these bad boys blow hers out of the water. Make them at the end of the roast cooking – Yorkies are best kept until the last minute for extra crispy, fluffiness.

Makes 12

3 **large eggs**
180ml/¾ cup **whole milk**
180g/6oz **plain flour**
a pinch of **salt**
100ml/scant ½ cup **vegetable oil**

1. Preheat the oven to 220°C/200°C fan/425°F/Gas 7.

2. Crack the eggs into a large bowl and use a balloon whisk to whisk until fluffy.

3. Pour in the milk and keep whisking, then whisk in the flour one third at a time. Keep whisking until you have a lump-free batter, then season with the pinch of salt. Transfer the batter to a jug for easy pouring, and leave it to rest for about 15 minutes.

4. Meanwhile, divide the vegetable oil equally between each hole of a 12-hole muffin tray (or use two 6-hole trays). Place the tray on to a baking sheet or into a baking tray (this is just to make it easy to move) and slide it into the oven for the oil to heat up while the batter rests.

5. Carefully remove the muffin tray on its baking sheet/tray from the oven, and pour equalish amounts of the batter mixture into the holes. Try your best not to get drips of the batter between the holes, as this can prevent the Yorkshires from rising.

6. Place the Yorkies into the oven and bake for 15 minutes – DON'T OPEN THE OVEN WHILE THEY ARE IN THERE – until they are risen, golden and crispy. Then serve them up, bab! x

← SEE HOW IT SHOULD LOOK

Honey Parsnip Crumble

Parsnips are the underrated vegetable of our generation... and that cannot continue any longer. This honey-parsnip-breadcrumb combo is made in heaven and will be the poster-child to get parsnips back on the map.

Serves 4–6

- 4–6 **parsnips**
- 2 tbsp **vegetable oil**
- 2 tbsp **Dijon mustard**
- 3 tbsp **runny honey**
- 3 **garlic cloves**, peeled and chopped
- 1 tsp **white wine vinegar**
- 1–3 tbsp **olive oil**
- 100g/3½oz **breadcrumbs** (I make my own chunky crumbs using stale bread)
- 2 **thyme sprigs**, leaves picked

1. Clean your parsnips (no need to peel), then trim off the tops and cut the parsnips in half lengthways.

2. Pour the vegetable oil into a saucepan wide enough to fit the parsnips and place over a medium–high heat. When hot, add the parsnips, cut sides down, and cook for 4 minutes, until the undersides are coloured.

3. Flip the parsnip halves over and cook for a further 4 minutes, until coloured on the curved sides, too. Remove from the pan on to a plate.

4. Add the mustard, the honey, two-thirds of the garlic and all the vinegar to the pan. Let this all come together and start bubbling, then tip the parsnips back into the pan and cook over a low heat for about 5–10 minutes, until they go a deep golden colour (but keep an eye that they don't burn).

5. Meanwhile, pour a little of the olive oil into a frying pan over a medium–high heat. Add the breadcrumbs, thyme leaves and the remaining garlic and keep stirring until the crumbs are golden and crispy.

6. Load the parsnips into a serving dish, then sprinkle the crumbs over the top and serve immediately. (If you're not ready to serve straight away, put the parsnips into the dish and keep warm in a low oven for up to about 20 minutes. Sprinkle the breadcrumbs over just before serving.)

SEE HOW IT SHOULD LOOK →

Butter-roasted Carrots

This is a petition to stop just cutting your carrots into circles and boiling them. The carrot deserves so much more! These whole carrots are cooked in butter, which brings out the flavour, adding a delicious, new carrot-y dimension. Goodbye carrot circles, hello butter-roasted carrots.

Serves 4–6

4–6 **carrots**
about 250g/9oz **butter**
1 **star anise**
a pinch of **cumin seeds**
a pinch of **flaky salt**

1. Peel your carrots, then trim off the tops, but leave the carrots whole.

2. Melt the butter in a saucepan that is big enough to hold the carrots in a single layer and add the star anise, cumin and salt. (You need enough butter to almost cover the carrots, so melt a bit more if you think it's looking too shallow.)

3. Tip in the carrots and cook over a low heat for about 20 minutes, until just tender (carefully poke in the end of a knife – if they are tender on the outside but still a little al dente in the middle, we are good to go).

4. Either, serve straight away; or, remove the carrots from the heat, leave them in the pan and set aside to cool as they are for about 1 hour. Just re-heat when needed.

Cauliflower Le Cheese

We all know Christmas 2020 was a weird one. The best thing about it for me was whapping out this cauliflower cheese and everyone saying it's the best they've ever had. It's cheesy, thick and rich (everything I aspire to be) and is worth cooking for every single roast dinner... ever.

Serves 4–6

- 1 recipe quantity of **Cheese Sauce** (see page 42)
- 1 tbsp **wholegrain mustard**
- 2 tsp **smoked paprika**
- 1 **cauliflower**
- 100g/3½oz **cheddar**, grated
- **black pepper**

1. Preheat the oven to 200°C/180°C fan/400°F/Gas 6.

2. Make or reheat your cheese sauce, adding the mustard and paprika, and seasoning with black pepper.

3. Remove the leaves from the cauliflower and cut off and discard any dodgy bits. Cut the cauliflower into medium-sized florets.

4. Tip the florets and leaves into an ovenproof dish (it's okay if they heap a bit), making a beautiful arrangement of cauli. Pour your cheese sauce over the top.

5. Sprinkle the grated cheese over and bake for 50 minutes, until golden on top, bubbling at the sides and the cauli is tender. Enjoy!

Braised Red Cabbage

This red cabbage is not just for Christmas. It adds a gorgeous sweetness to your roast and it's my go-to to bring the whole meal together. I love cabbage… whether it's battered (like earlier on in the book) or pickled or braised. Mmmm… pickled cabbage. Let me just think about that for a while.

Serves 4–6

½ **small red cabbage**
3 tbsp **light brown soft sugar**
3 tbsp **red wine vinegar**
25g/1oz **butter**
1 **cinnamon stick**
a pinch of **chilli flakes**

1. Cut out the stalk from your cabbage and slice the cabbage into four pieces. Then finely slice each piece.

2. Place the slices into a large saucepan over a medium heat. Add all the remaining ingredients and give it all a good stir.

3. Put the lid on the pan and leave the cabbage to cook for about 30 minutes, stirring occasionally, until tender. If you're not ready to serve immediately, leave the lid on and the cabbage over a low heat to keep warm for about 1 hour.

← SEE HOW IT SHOULD LOOK

Sweet

Pastry

Sweet Pastry

Sweet pastry makes me think of grandmas. It's the smell of an apple pie on the windowsill that you see in cartoons. It's a warm hug that just keeps coming. I'm always down for a pastry snuggle.

Makes enough for 2 large pies (lid and base) or 3 large tarts (base only)
- 500g/1lb 2oz **plain flour**
- 90g/3oz **icing sugar**
- 45g/1½oz **ground almonds**
- 300g/10oz **butter**, cubed and chilled
- 1 **egg**, beaten with 1 **egg yolk**, then chilled
- 1–2 tbsp **ice-cold water**

1. Using your hands, a food processor or a stand mixer, combine the flour, icing sugar, ground almonds and butter. Either: with your hands, rub the ingredients between your thumbs and fingertips; or in a food processor, use the pulse function; in a stand mixer, use the paddle attachment and add the butter a few cubes at a time. Whatever the method, keep going until you have fine breadcrumbs.

2. If you're working by hand, make a well in the centre of the flour mixture, add the egg mixture, then the ice-cold water as necessary (just enough so that the dough starts to clump and bind), and work quickly to incorporate. If you're using a food processor or stand mixer, add the eggs, pulse or mix, then add the water a little at a time. Once the dough starts to clump, tip it out and bring it together briefly by hand. Don't overwork it, otherwise the pastry will be elastic, rather than crisp.

3. Divide the dough into 3 equal pieces and form each into a ball. Press the balls with the palm of your hand to turn each into a fairly flat, but fat disc (this will just help with rolling whenever you come to use the pastry). Wrap the pastry discs tightly in cling film and leave them in the fridge to rest for at least 30 minutes before using, or before freezing (see below).

[STORAGE: FREEZER **3 MONTHS** (RAW, WRAPPED) / DEFROST FOR 4 HOURS OR OVERNIGHT IN THE FRIDGE BEFORE USING]

Strawberry Tart

I love this tart. I'm never that fussy about 'pretty' food. Like I always found dropping edible flowers on desserts at work a bit... flowery. I'm much more of a flavour girl. Get me messy with buffalo wings and blue cheese any day. Except, that is, on the day I'm making this.

This is not a chicken-wing pie – this is a strawberry tart filled with delicious crème-patissière, and here pretty works... it's simple, but beautiful and has the flavours to match. You can use a mixture of fruit on the top if you prefer – a combo of sliced strawberries and nectarines, blueberries and raspberries works well. Whatever you fancy. The result reminds me of those gorgeous tarts you see in the windows of pastry shops when you're on holiday. You buy one, and then you're worried about how you'll go about eating it on the move while also sweating in the European sun. The answer? Make a huge one at home, get geared up with the appropriate cutlery and just dive in as you please. Slices are nice and everything, but why not just dig into the middle with your fork and have a really good forkin' time?

TURN OVER →

→ STRAWBERRY TART

Serves 6–8

The core
⅓ recipe quantity of **Sweet Pastry** (see page 182)

For the crème pat
1 tbsp **plain flour**, plus extra for dusting
butter, for greasing
350ml/1½ cups **whole milk**
½ tsp **vanilla extract**
4 **large egg yolks**
1 tbsp **cornflour**
5 tbsp **caster sugar**

To decorate
about 2 punnets of **strawberries** (about 50 strawberries), hulled
2 tbsp **apricot jam**, to glaze

1. Lightly dust your work surface with flour. Roll out the pastry to a disc about 30cm/12 inches in diameter and 3mm/⅛ inch thick. Carefully transfer the disc to the tart tin and let it sink into the hollow. Tear off a little piece of pastry, roll it into a ball and use to press the pastry disc into the corner around the base, and up the side to create a wall. Make sure there are no gaps or holes. Use a knife to trim any overhang. Transfer to the fridge to chill for 30 minutes.

2. Meanwhile, preheat the oven to 190°C/170°C fan/375°F/Gas 5. Grease a 23cm/9 inch loose-bottomed, fluted tart tin with a little butter.

3. Now we are going to blind bake the tart case. First, using a fork, poke holes in rows all over the bottom of the tart case and line the pastry with a big piece of scrunched-up baking paper so that it covers the bottom and sides. Then, load up with baking beans or dried beans (see tip, page 120).

4. Bake the tart case like this for 15 minutes, until it's just browning. Remove it from the oven and, using the edges of the baking paper to help you, take out the baking paper and beans.

5. Return the pastry case to the oven for about 10–15 minutes, until it is golden brown all over. Leave to cool while you make the filling.

6. Get a deep tray or bowl and place a sieve on top.

7. Place the milk and vanilla in a medium saucepan and put that over a high heat. Bring to the boil, then remove from the heat.

8. Meanwhile, in a separate bowl, whisk together the egg yolks, cornflour, plain flour and caster sugar until pale, fluffy and thick.

9. Pour one quarter of the hot milk into the egg mixture, whisking continuously, then pour this mixture back into the hot milk in the saucepan and place it over a low heat. Using a spatula, stir continuously so that the eggs don't scramble, and cook for about 7–10 minutes, until you have a thick and smooth custard (see tip, page 200).

10. Strain the thickened custard through the sieve into the tray or bowl and cover the surface with cling film (make sure it's actually touching the surface), which will stop a skin forming. Put this in the fridge to chill for 30 minutes, until thickened.

11. Pour the chilled filling into the cooled tart case, then cover the surface again with cling film and chill in the fridge for a further 2 hours, until set (you can get it out sooner, but it will be soft).

12. Starting at the middle, and working outwards in circles, decorate with all the whole strawberries (or make any which pattern you fancy).

13. Warm the apricot jam and 2 tablespoons of water in a pan over a low heat or in the microwave until runny enough to brush. Brush this over the strawberries to glaze, then chill until you're ready to serve.

Pop's Pop Tarts

My little brother, CJ, and sister, Trix, introduced me to ready-made pop tarts – I'm the much-older sister so was in my teens when they were little and pop tarts were the new thing from the US. Pop tarts are fun and they're different, and when you realise how easy they are to whip up at home, you're winning!

Makes 6

The core
⅓ recipe quantity of **Sweet Pastry** (see page 182)

For the pop tarts
plain flour, for dusting
8 tbsp **strawberry jam**
1 **egg,** beaten

For the topping
5 tbsp **icing sugar**
4 tsp **sugar sprinkles**

1. Lightly flour your work surface. Divide the pastry in half and roll out each piece to a large rectangle, about 3mm/⅛ thick. Cut each pastry rectangle into 6 small rectangles (about 15cm/6 inches by 10cm/4 inches) to give you 12 rectangles of pastry altogether.

2. Put 1 rounded tablespoon of strawberry jam into the centre of 6 of the rectangles and then gently spread it out using the back of the spoon, leaving about a 1cm/½ inch border all the way around the edge.

3. Using a pastry brush, lightly egg wash the border of each rectangle, around the jam, and place a plain rectangle on top, using a fork to seal the pastry edges together all the way around. Repeat for all the rectangles.

4. Using your brush again, egg wash the outside of your pastry parcels. Then, with a skewer make 6 little holes on top of each pastry parcel (just so the steam can escape). Now you have pop tarts!

5. Place the pop tarts on a baking tray lined with baking paper and chill them in the fridge for 25 minutes to firm up. Meanwhile, preheat the oven to 190°C/170°C fan/375°F/Gas 5.

6. Once the pop tarts are chilled, bake them for 30 minutes, until just golden and a little crispy. Remove from the oven and transfer them to a wire rack to cool completely.

7. Make the topping by tipping the icing sugar into a bowl and adding water just a drop at a time, until you have a thick, smooth consistency.

8. Spread the icing over the cooled pop tarts, then scatter over the sugar sprinkles.

Sweet Potato Pie

You were thinking it... how is she going to bring potatoes into a sweet pie? And I've only gone and done it! Everyone reading in North America will be, like, 'Of course! What else?' In the UK, not so much. We need to appreciate this American classic more in the UK, I think. Once you've tasted your first sweet potato pie, you will never look back. It's hard to explain the flavour and texture – the results are kind of a delicious, sweet, custardy dessert that's almost like an egg custard, but without the egg and just potato heaven instead. If you need to trust me when it comes to trying one dish that so far you're unsure about, this one is it. It's so simple, so tasty, and will forever change the way you view a sweet potato.

If you've got picky eaters, make this dessert incognito and tell them afterwards what it is. It's so good they'll want it again and again. Main tip: appropriate portion control – you'll need enough for seconds or thirds.

TURN OVER →

→ SWEET POTATO PIE

Serves 6

The core
⅓ recipe quantity of **Sweet Pastry** (see page 182)

For the filling
plain flour, for dusting
butter, for greasing
2 **sweet potatoes**
1 x 397g/14oz tin of **condensed milk**
3 tbsp **caster sugar**
2 **large eggs**
1 tsp **lemon juice**
1 tsp **ground cinnamon**
½ teaspoon **ground nutmeg**
a pinch of **salt**
1 bag of **mini marshmallows**

1. Lightly flour your work surface. Roll out the pastry to a disc about 30cm/ 12 inches in diameter and 3mm/⅛ inch thick. Carefully transfer the disc to the tart tin and let it sink into the hollow. Tear off a little piece of pastry, roll it into a ball and use it to gently press the pastry disc into the corner around the base, and up the side to create a wall. Make sure there are no gaps or holes. Use a knife to trim any overhanging pastry. Transfer to the fridge to chill for 30 minutes.

2. Meanwhile, preheat the oven to 190°C/170°C fan/375°F/Gas 5. Grease a 20cm/8 inch loose-bottomed, fluted tart tin with a little butter.

3. Now we are going to blind bake the tart case. First, using a fork, poke holes in rows all over the bottom of the tart case and line the pastry with a big piece of scrunched-up baking paper so that it covers the bottom and sides. Then, load up with baking beans or dried beans (see tip, page 120).

4. Bake the tart case like this for 15 minutes, until it's just browning. Remove it from the oven and, using the edges of the baking paper to help you, take out the baking paper and beans.

5. Return the pastry case to the oven for about 7–10 minutes, until the bottom is slightly browned, too. Leave to cool while you make the filling. Leave the oven on.

6. Pierce the sweet potatoes with a fork and place them on the racks in the oven. Cook for 45 minutes to 1 hour, until soft and cooked through (you can start this while the tart case is blind baking, if you like; or cook them in the microwave, one at a time, for 6 minutes each at full power). Leave the oven on.

7. Let the potatoes cool for 15 minutes, then cut them in half and scoop out the flesh into a bowl. Weigh the flesh and measure out 400g/14oz (eat any leftovers).

8. Mash the 400g/14oz of sweet potato well and add the condensed milk. Using a hand-held stick blender or a food processor, blitz the mixture into a smooth purée, then stir in all the remaining ingredients, except the marshmallows.

9. Spoon the filling into your cooled tart case and bake for 40–50 minutes, until a little puffed up, but set in the middle. Remove from the oven and leave to cool completely (about 2 hours).

10. Preheat the grill to medium, then carefully arrange your mini marshmallows one by one in circles around the top of the tart. Place the tart under the grill for a few minutes, until the marshmallows are melted, golden and gooey. Serve for an all-American feast.

Cherry Bakewell Cheesecake

True story: last year, my friends Lucy, Haz, their Shih Tzu-cross-pug Bella, my boyfriend, my pugs Kipper and Krypto and I travelled all the way to Bakewell JUST to have an original Bakewell pudding. All in the name of research, of course. It was 100% worth the journey and I'd recommend you never question travelling for a good bit of cake. This is a twist on the Bakewell classic and is my favourite cheesecake of all time. It uses a pastry base alongside a cherry filling and cream cheese galore. The cheesecake needs overnight to set, so start it the day before you intend to serve it up in all its glory. I ate a slice of this every day for ten days and it was the best ten days of my life. See you in ten days' time.

Serves 6–10

The core
⅓ recipe quantity of **Sweet Pastry** (see page 182)

For the frangipane
125g/4½oz **butter**, at room temperature, plus extra for greasing
25g/1oz **plain flour**, plus extra for dusting
125g/4½oz **icing sugar**
125g/4½oz **ground almonds**
2 **large eggs**

For the filling
1 x 410g/14oz tin of **black cherry pie filling** (not cherries in syrup)
340g/12oz **full-fat cream cheese**
500g/1lb 2oz **mascarpone**
100g/3½oz **caster sugar**
1 tsp **vanilla extract**
300ml/1¼ cups **double cream**

To decorate
10 **glacé cherries**, halved
10 **whole cherries**, with stalks
100g/3½oz **flaked almonds**, toasted

1. Grease a 23cm/9 inch springform cake tin (4cm/1½ inches deep) with a little butter.

2. Lightly flour your work surface and roll out the pastry to a disc about 30cm/12 inches in diameter and 3mm/⅛ inch thick. Carefully transfer the disc to the cake tin and let it sink into the hollow. Tear off a little piece of pastry, roll it into a ball and use it to gently press the pastry case into the corner around the base, and so that it comes halfway (2cm/¾ inch) up the side of the tin. In the end, the cheesecake filling will come up above the edge of the pastry.

3. Prick the pastry base all over with a fork and line it with a big piece of scrunched-up baking paper. Then, load up with baking beans or dried beans (see tip, page 120). Transfer it to the fridge to chill for 30 minutes.

4. Meanwhile, preheat the oven to 190°C/170°C fan/375°F/Gas 5. Once the pastry has chilled, blind bake the case for 15 minutes, until it's just browning.

5. While the pastry case is in the oven, make your frangipane. Using a hand whisk, whisk the butter in a mixing bowl until it is fluffy and light. Then, add the icing sugar and ground almonds and mix until combined. One at a time, add the eggs, mixing well between each addition, then finish by folding in the flour until all incorporated. Set aside.

6. Remove the pie crust from the oven (leave the oven on). Remove the baking beans and baking paper, then pour half the cherry filling into the crust, spreading the cherries out all the way to the edge in an even layer. (Chill the remaining cherry filling – you can use it to decorate, if you like.)

7. Spoon all the frangipane mixture on top of the cherry filling in the crust, smoothing it out evenly to cover. Return the tart to the oven for a further 25–30 minutes, until the frangipane is golden but still a little soft to touch.

8. While the tart is baking, in a bowl and using a hand whisk, whisk together the cream cheese, mascarpone, sugar and vanilla, until light. Pour in the double cream and whisk again until smooth and fully combined.

9. Remove the pastry and frangipane base from the oven. Place the tin on a wire rack and allow to cool completely (about 1–2 hours).

10. Cover the cooled base with your cream cheese and mascarpone topping, then leave in the fridge overnight, until set.

11. Remove the cheesecake from the springform tin and decorate with the remaining half of the cherry filling, if you like, as well as the glacé cherries, fresh whole cherries, and the toasted flaked almonds.

SEE HOW IT SHOULD LOOK →

custard

Perfect Custard

I'm going out on a limb here, but... there's nothing that can beat homemade custard. Forget the powder. Fresh, homemade custard is rich, delicious and, well, homely. It's everything you want to cover all over your dessert. And I mean ALL over. None of this 'there's-not-enough' situation. Make it fresh. And make lots of it. No complaints.

Makes 1½ jam jars
- 300ml/1¼ cups **double cream**
- ¼ tsp **vanilla extract**
- 3 **egg yolks**
- 3 tbsp **caster sugar**

1. Get yourself set up. If you are not using the custard immediately, then you will need something big enough for the custard to be strained into. If you are using the custard straight away, place a sieve over a jug, or whatever it is you're serving it in.

2. Pour the double cream into a small saucepan and add the vanilla. Place the pan over a medium heat and slowly bring it up to the simmer – just so that bubbles are forming around the edges of the cream. Remove the pan from the heat and set aside.

3. In a bowl, beat together the egg yolks and sugar, until the colour has turned pale.

4. Stirring the whole time, little by little, pour about half the cream from the pan into the sweetened yolks – this will gently bring the yolks up to temperature so that they don't scramble when they go into the rest of the hot cream.

5. Then, pour the yolk mixture in the bowl into the pan with the remaining cream and return to a low–medium heat, stirring continuously for about 7–10 minutes, until the custard thickens enough to coat the back of a spoon. *TIP!

6. Strain the thickened custard through the sieve into your chosen receptacle. If you're keeping it until later, cover the surface of the custard with cling film (make sure it's actually touching the surface), which will stop a skin forming on top.

*CHEF'S TIP
To check your eggs are cooked in a custard or a curd, dip in a spoon. When the sauce is thick enough to coat the back of the spoon, run your finger across it. If you get a clean line with no dribbling, the eggs are done!

[STORAGE: **FRIDGE** 3 DAYS]

Butterscotch Apple Crumble

Apple crumble is *the* staple of British desserts. It's good just as it comes, but I think I've unlocked the next level in the game of crumbles – with the butterscotch, which cuts through the tartness. Get me a spoon.

Serves 4–6

The core
1 recipe quantity of **Perfect Custard** (see page 200)

For the topping
150g/5¼oz **plain flour**
90g/3oz **dark brown soft sugar**
a pinch of **salt**
100g/3½oz **butter**, cubed and chilled

For the filling
50g/2oz **butter**
150g/5¼oz **dark brown soft sugar**
100ml/scant ½ cup **double cream**
¼ tsp **vanilla extract**
2 **large cooking apples**, peeled, cored and sliced
a large pinch of **flaky salt**

1. Preheat the oven to 190°C/170°C fan/375°F/Gas 5.

2. Make the topping. Mix the flour, sugar and salt in a large bowl. Then, a few cubes at a time, add the butter, using your thumbs and fingertips to rub it in until it looks like lovely, chunky breadcrumbs (you don't want it too fine – some lumps are good for extra crunch once it's cooked). Set aside.

3. Make the filling. Place the butter in a medium saucepan over a medium heat. Leave to melt, then add the sugar and stir. Leave to dissolve, stirring every so often, just so that the caramel doesn't burn. Meanwhile, pour the cream into a jug and stir in the vanilla.

4. After about 3–5 minutes, reduce the heat under the pan to low and, using a whisk, carefully pour in the vanilla cream, whisking as you go.

5. Add the apples and flaky salt, and gently stir them through so that the apple slices are completely coated in the thick butterscotch. Transfer this mixture into a medium oven dish.

6. Scatter the crumble evenly over the top. Bake for 30–40 minutes, or until the crumble is golden and the filling is bubbling.

7. While the crumble is in the oven, warm up your custard: place it in a saucepan over a low heat, stirring continuously, for about 5 minutes, until it's warm and silky. Be patient – don't rush it, as we don't want it to split.

8. Serve the hot crumble in bowls smothered in lashings of custard – and vanilla ice cream, because I love it with that, too. So, yes, both.

Bananas and Custard French Toast

First, an apology to my friend Martha. We've been best friends since we were three, but there's always been a third wheel in the relationship... Martha's fear of bananas. I'd like to think that this brunch might turn her around, but it probably won't. So, sorry Martha, it's incredible and I couldn't leave it out.

Serves 2

The core
1 recipe quantity of **Perfect Custard** (see page 200)

For the French toast
100ml/scant ½ cup **whole milk**
4 tbsp **caster sugar**
2 **bananas**, peeled, and sliced lengthways in half
1 tsp **vegetable oil**
4 x 2.5cm-thick (1 inch) slices of **brioche loaf**
4 tbsp **crunchy peanut butter**
a knob of **butter**
2 tbsp chopped **salted peanuts**
a spoonful of **mixed berries** (optional), to serve

1. Pour the custard into a bowl or oven dish that's large enough to dip in your brioche slices. Mix the milk into your custard just to loosen it slightly.

2. Tip the sugar on to a plate and roll the banana halves through so that it sticks on both sides.

3. Heat the vegetable oil in a large, non-stick frying pan over a medium heat. Add the bananas and fry for about 4–5 minutes each side, until golden and caramelised all over. Remove from the pan and set aside for later. Keep the pan to hand.

4. On one edge of each slice of brioche, using a paring (small chopping) knife, slice through the thickness to make a pocket inside. Use a teaspoon to fill the pockets with equal amounts of delicious peanut butter.

5. Dip the filled slices into your custard, carefully turning each slice to coat it on both sides.

6. Add the knob of butter to the frying pan and place it over a low–medium heat. When the butter starts melting, place your soggy, filled brioche slices into the pan (do this in batches, if necessary).

7. Fry for about 2 minutes on each side, just so that the bread is golden and toasted to the point of getting a little crisp around the edges. Remove from the pan and transfer to a serving plate.

8. Top with the caramelised bananas, chopped peanuts, berries (if using) and a good dollop of leftover (controversial) cold custard. Offt! Yes, please!

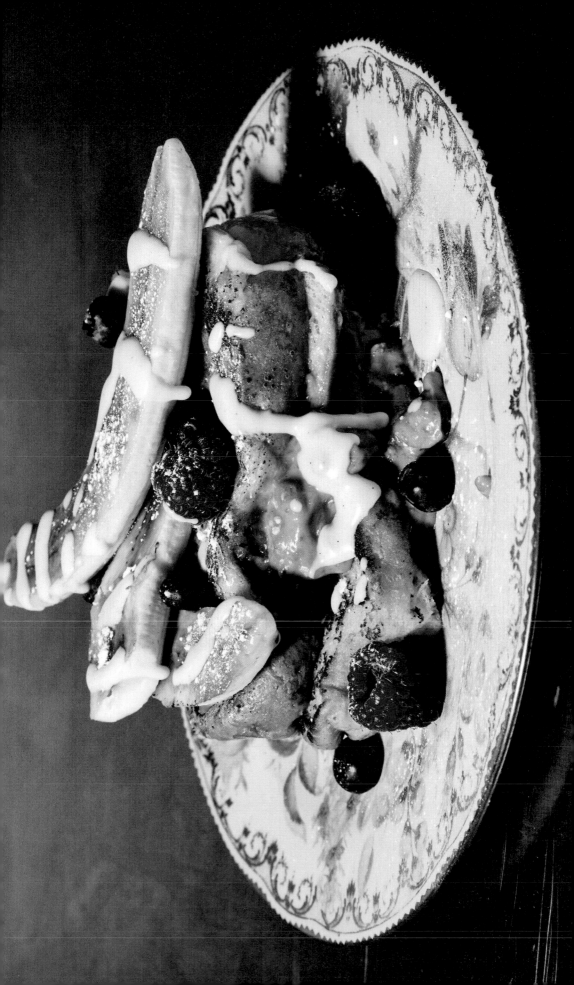

Custard Spudnuts

My favourite word in this book... spudnuts. I discovered the potato doughnut during my 25 days of potato recipes – they're a big thing in North America and I'm putting money on spudnut stalls making their way over to the UK soon. Or, maybe I'll just start that myself. Try them and let me know if you're willing to invest in Poppy's Spuddy Nuts (might need to work on the name...).

Now, I promise these doughnuts don't taste like mashed potato. The starch adds a rich thickness to the dough that makes for a beautifully textured result. Fill that with custard and Bob's your uncle, Fanny's your aunt – the perfect spudnut now exists. Feel free to play around with the fillings. I've gone with custard. But why not squirt them full of jam? Or custard and jam? Maybe your favourite chocolate spread? Or even all three? I would love to see your creations for myself. Tag me in all your spudnuts.

TURN OVER →

→ CUSTARD SPUDNUTS

Makes 10–12

The core
1 recipe quantity of **Perfect Custard** (see page 200)

For the spudnuts
1 large **maris piper potato**, peeled, and cut into 1cm/½ inch chunks
1 tbsp **salt**, for the cooking water, plus 1 tsp
180ml/¾ cup **whole milk**
60g/2oz **butter**
3 rounded tbsp **caster sugar**
a pinch of **gound nutmeg**
a little squeeze of **lemon** juice
1½ tsp **active dried yeast**
2 **eggs**, beaten
1 tsp **vanilla extract**
400g/14oz **plain flour**, plus extra for dusting
1 litre **vegetable oil**, for deep-frying

For the vanilla glaze
6 tbsp **icing sugar**
3 tbsp **warm water**
a pinch of **cream of tartar**
1 tsp **vanilla extract**
2 tbsp **liquid glucose**

*CHEF'S TIP
If you don't have a piping bag, use a plastic sandwich bag and simply trim off a corner to give you a hole the size that you need, then you're on your way!

1. Tip the potato chunks into a large saucepan and just cover with water. Add the tablespoon of salt. Place the pan over a high heat and bring to the boil. Boil for 10 minutes, until the potatoes slide off when you poke them with the point of a knife. Drain them in a colander, suspend the colander in the potato pan and cover with a tea towel for 10 minutes, until the potatoes have steamed off. Tip the potatoes back into the pan and mash until smooth.

2. Stir half the milk, and the butter, sugar, nutmeg and lemon juice and the teaspoon of salt into the pan with the hot mash. Leave to cool completely (about 15 minutes).

3. While the mash is cooling, warm the remaining half of the milk in a small pan over a low heat until just body temperature (it should feel lukewarm when you put your finger in it). Pour this into a jug and combine it with the yeast. Leave to ferment for 5–10 minutes – it should go nice and frothy to show that your yeast is getting busy.

4. Tip the eggs into a large bowl with the vanilla and beat them together (you can do this in a stand mixer with the paddle attachment if you have one). Add the cold potato mixture and the activated milky yeast.

5. Add half the flour to the bowl and beat to a smooth paste, then, one third at a time, add the remaining flour, beating well between each addition.

6. Knead the potato mixture until formed into a soft dough (either in a stand mixer with the dough hook or on your work surface by hand). Cover and leave to rise in a warm place for 1–2 hours, until doubled in size.

7. On a floured work surface, punch down your risen dough to knock out the air. Then, use a rolling pin to roll it out to about 2.5cm/1 inch thick.

8. Using the floured rim of a mug or wine glass, stamp out 10–12 round shapes (don't cut out a middle – we're making filled rather than ring spudnuts). Cover, then prove for 30–40 minutes, until puffed and airy. (You can make a few extra from the offcuts, if you like.)

9. Meanwhile, load your custard into a medium piping bag fitted with a small plain nozzle. Twist the opening and at the point just above the nozzle to stop the custard escaping for now, then set aside. *TIP!

10. Make the glaze by combining all the glaze ingredients in a bowl and set that aside, too.

11. Towards the end of the proving time, pour your oil into a large, deep pan to about 10–15cm/4–6 inches deep. Place it over a high heat and heat until it reaches 175–180°C/345–350°F on a cooking thermometer (or until a tiny bit of dough dropped into the oil sizzles and turns golden within 60 seconds).

12. Once the doughnuts are ready, add them 2 or 3 at a time into the hot oil, using a long-handled spoon to gently turn them for 4 minutes altogether, until golden and puffy all over. Set aside each batch to drain and cool on kitchen paper while you deep-fry the next.

13. Once the doughnuts are cool enough to handle, use a skewer or a knife to make a small hole in the side of each. Untwist your piping bag and stuff your nozzle into those holes to pipe in your custard. Dunk the doughnuts into the glaze, leave the glaze to set a little (about 5 minutes), then enjoy!

Forget-the-Crème Brûlées

I'm often asked if there's anything I don't enjoy eating. Confession: I hate jelly. The texture, nah. I'm out. Goodbye. Sometimes crème brûlées can have that kinda texture and I'm not a fan. This one, however, does not. Make your custard fresh for this recipe, because at the point you think you're done, you'll need to go a bit further. Get your ramekins ready before you start.

Makes 2

The core
1 recipe quantity of **Perfect Custard** (see page 200), but only up to Step 5

For the topping
100g/3½oz **granulated sugar**

1. So, you're making your custard and you've got to Step 5 where you're cooking for 7–10 minutes, until the custard coats the back of a spoon. Now, what we're going to do is risky, but it pays off: keep cooking for an extra 4 minutes (11–14 minutes in total), to get a super-thick, almost-set custard.

2. Pour this through a sieve directly into your two ramekins. Then, cover the surface of each portion with cling film (make sure it's actually touching the surface), which will stop a skin forming. Move the ramekins to the fridge and leave the custards for 2 hours, until set. (Actually, 6 hours or overnight setting is better – if you have/can wait that long.)

3. Meanwhile, make the caramel for the top. (Using caramel instead of sugar is a trick I learned at work. It's quicker to melt and less likely to burn.) Tip the sugar into a small, heavy-based saucepan and add enough water to just cover. Place the pan over a medium–high heat and leave it. Don't stir it, don't move it, just let it do its thing for 5–6 minutes, until it is light brown.

4. For something to do in the meantime, place a large sheet of baking paper on your work surface – it needs to be big enough to cope with your caramel without it running off the edges (put it inside a large baking tray, if you like).

5. Remove the light brown caramel from the heat and very carefully pour it on to the baking paper. Leave it to cool and set for about 10 minutes. DO NOT TOUCH IT. IT'S HOT!

6. Once the caramel is completely cool, remove it from the baking paper, break it up and put it into your food processor. Blitz it to a powder.

7. Once the custards are set, get them out of the fridge and sprinkle a tablespoon of the powdered caramel on top of each. Then, if you have a kitchen blow torch, fire that up; if not, preheat the grill (broiler, if you're in North America) to medium and heat away for 2–3 minutes, until the tops are melted and golden. Leave for a minute to harden until crackable, then serve.

Mering

ue

French Meringue

Meringues are just classy aren't they? They make me feel proper posh and accomplished when I've whipped together my peaks and nailed the results. It's like riding a bike, when you've got the balance just right, you'll be jumping in the saddle at every opportunity.

Makes 1 pavlova nest or about 6 small nests or about 60 meringue kisses

4 **large egg whites**
250g/9oz **caster sugar** (**superfine sugar** for my North American friends)
1 tsp **white wine vinegar**
1 tsp **cornflour**

1. Preheat the oven to 120°C/100°C fan/235°F/Gas ¾ for individual nests or meringue kisses. Or 150°C/130°C fan/300°F/Gas 2 for a pavlova nest.

2. Tip the egg whites into a clean bowl and, using an electric hand-held whisk or a stand mixer with the whisk attachment, whisk the egg whites on medium speed to a stiff peak... put that bowl upside down over your head and if you're not covered in slosh at the end, then they're at stiff peak.

3. Continue whisking (still on medium speed) and add in the sugar, 1 tablespoon at a time, leaving each to mix in before adding the next.

4. Once all the sugar is in, continue to whisk for a further 3–4 minutes, until the meringue is glossy and thick.

5. Mix the vinegar and cornflour together in a small bowl and, using a spatula, fold the mixture into the meringue. Fold until just combined, taking care not to overmix (overmixing can knock the air out). At this stage, if you're not using the meringue mixture for one of the recipes in this chapter, use the tip below for a simple way to cook and EAT!

> ***CHEF'S TIP**
>
> Use 2 tablespoons to scoop and transfer dollops of the meringue (about 6) on to a baking tray lined with baking paper. Use the back of the spoon to turn the dollops into nests. Bake at the lower temperature for 1¼ hours, until crisp on the outside and slightly gooey in the middle. Leave to cool in the oven, heat turned off and with the door slightly ajar. Delicious with whipped cream and fruit, just like that. For the meringue kisses (about 60), bake at the lower temperature for about 1 hour. Cool on wire racks.

[STORAGE: RAW **NO STORAGE** / BAKED NESTS + KISSES IN AN AIRTIGHT CONTAINER AT ROOM TEMPERATURE **3 DAYS**]

Italian Meringue

Okay, so are you ready to take your meringue game to the next level? Italian meringue is a bit more complex than its French cousin, because it requires a bit of sugar work and temperature control along the way. But, let's be honest, if there's anything worth dedicating your time to, it's how to best work your sugar. It's like homework with delicious meringue at the end of it. If this had been on the curriculum, I probably wouldn't have failed everything.

Makes 1 large tart topping or about 6 small nests or about 50 meringue kisses

250g/9oz **caster sugar** (**superfine sugar** for my North American friends)
2 **egg whites**

1. Tip the sugar into a small saucepan and add 110ml/7 tbsp plus 1 tsp of water. Place over a medium heat and give the pan a little swirl to combine, but DO NOT stir.

2. Leave the sugar to dissolve to a thick syrup. Once the temperature of the syrup is 100°C/212°F on a sugar thermometer, tip your egg whites into a clean bowl and start whisking (using an electric handheld whisk or a stand mixer with the whisk attachment on medium speed).

3. Whisk the egg whites to stiff peaks – you're aiming to get them to this point by the time the sugar syrup reaches 118°C/244°F on the thermometer. If the eggs peak too soon, wait for the sugar to get to temperature before continuing.

4. Once the syrup is ready, get your eggs whisking on a medium–high speed and then, very carefully and slowly, trickle the sugar syrup down the inside of the bowl into the whites.

5. Once all the syrup is in, keep whisking until the meringue has cooled to body temperature (if you're using a stand mixer, you can test this simply by placing your hand on the side of the bowl; otherwise, take a teaspoonful out of the bowl and test the temperature with your finger).

6. Spoon the meringue into a piping bag (twist the opening and just above the nozzle to stop it oozing out) and use immediately, or store it as below.

[STORAGE: RAW **IN THE FREEZER IN A PIPING BAG FOR 2-3 HOURS ONLY** / BRING BACK TO ROOM TEMP 30 MINUTES BEFORE USING]

Pat's Pav (On Tour)

Pat is my stepdad's grandma, but step-great-grandma is a bit of a mouthful, so I've always just called her Grandma. There's no surprise that an 11-year-old, overweight little girl and a Grandma who loved making desserts bonded so quickly. Plus, her pavlova was a standout at any birthday buffet. I have decided to take the classic on tour with tropical fruits in preference to the more usual strawberries, as I do try and get in as many of my five-a-day as I can (especially if they're covered in cream and meringue...).

Serves 4–6

The core
1 recipe quantity of **French Meringue** (see page 214)

For the filling
300ml/1¼ cups **double cream**
¼ tsp **vanilla extract**
3 tbsp **icing sugar**, plus extra for dusting
2 **passion fruits**
2 **kiwis**, peeled, some sliced, some diced small
½ **pineapple**, peeled, cored, and diced small
1 **mango**, peeled, destoned, and diced small

1. Preheat the oven to 130°C/110°C fan/250°F/Gas 1. Line a baking tray with baking paper.

2. Spoon about two thirds of your meringue on to the lined baking tray and gently spread it into a disc – a big round of about 20cm/8 inches in diameter. Spoon the remaining meringue around the edge of the disc to make a rim (this will hold your fruit once the meringue is cooked).

3. Bake the meringue disc for 1 hour, until crisp on the outside and gooey in the middle, then turn the oven off and open the door slightly. Leave the disc to cool in the oven like this for about 1 hour. (After this, if you aren't constructing your pav straight away, as long as it's completely cool, wrap it in cling film and store it at room temperature for up to 3 days.)

4. While the meringue is cooling, make a Chantilly cream (fancy name for a sweetened, fluffy cream). Using a balloon whisk, in a bowl whisk together the double cream, vanilla and icing sugar for about 10 minutes, until soft and pillowy. (Doing this by hand means you'll be less likely to over-whisk the cream so that it starts to look crumbly.) Cover the bowl and put the cream in the fridge until you're ready to construct your pavlova.

5. Halve the passion fruits and use a spoon to scoop out the seeds into a large bowl. Add all the other fruits, mix to distribute everything evenly, then cover and leave in the fridge until you need them.

6. To build the pav, set the meringue disc on a serving plate and spoon on your whipped Chantilly cream, nice and high. Pile on the tropical fruit salad, making sure some of that juice runs off the edge... (my mouth is watering). Dust with icing sugar and serve up immediately.

Eton Mess Pancakes

Two of the best things in the world come together for the perfect brunch. Imagine your favourite pancakes. And then imagine everything you love about an Eton mess - meringue, strawberries, cream. It's literally perfect.

Makes 9

The core
any leftover baked **French meringue** (see page 214), broken into pieces

For the pancakes
270g/9½oz **plain flour**
a big pinch of **salt**
6 tbsp **caster sugar**
2 tsp **baking powder**
2 **large eggs**, lightly beaten
260ml/generous 1 cup **whole milk**
60g/2oz **unsalted butter**, melted and cooled

For the topping
100ml/scant ½ cup **double cream**
¼ tsp **vanilla extract**
3 tbsp **icing sugar**, plus extra for dusting
400g/14oz **strawberries**, hulled and quartered

1. Preheat the oven to 150°C/130°C fan/300°F/Gas 2.

2. In a bowl, mix together the flour, salt, sugar and baking powder. Set aside. Pour the eggs and the milk into a jug and add the melted butter. Stir to combine. Carefully pour the wet mixture into the dry and use a fork or whisk to mix everything together, until completely smooth.

3. Place a dry, non-stick frying pan over a medium heat and leave it to warm up for a couple of minutes. Once the pan is warm enough that a drop of batter colours within 45–60 seconds, add a ladleful of the pancake mixture. Leave it to spread naturally (no need to move it in any way) and cook for about 2–3 minutes, until you can see bubbles appearing all over the surface. Flip the pancake and cook the other side for 2–3 minutes, until golden.

4. Transfer the cooked pancake to a baking tray and place in the oven to keep warm. Repeat, cooking the pancakes in batches of 1 or 2 at a time, depending on the size of your pan. You should get about 9 altogether.

5. While the pancakes are in the oven, make a Chantilly cream (fancy name for a sweetened, fluffy cream). Using a balloon whisk, in a bowl whisk together the double cream, the vanilla and 1 tablespoon of the icing sugar for about 10 minutes, until soft and pillowy. Set aside.

6. In a separate bowl, toss your strawbs with the remaining icing sugar.

7. Now build: place a pancake on a serving plate, top with a spoonful of strawbs, a spoonful of cream and some crumbled meringue. Slap on another pancake and repeat to create a stack. I can't eat more than 2 in a stack, but go ahead and stack them higher if you can. Dust with icing sugar and serve.

S'mores Dauphine

These little nuggets of heaven are going to bring you over the line on our potato-appreciation journey. Impress your mates, then tell them it's potato.

Makes 9 (serves 2 or 3)

The core
½ recipe quantity of **Italian Meringue** (see page 216)

For the dough
2 **maris piper potatoes**, peeled, and cut into 1cm/½ inch chunks
1 tbsp **salt**, for the cooking water
20g/⅔oz **unsalted butter,** plus an extra 10g/⅓oz softened
2 tbsp **whole milk**
1 tbsp **any white sugar**
2½ tbsp **plain flour,** plus extra for dusting
1 **large egg**
about 500ml/2 cups **vegetable oil**, for deep-frying
5–7 tbsp **chocolate spread**

1. Tip the potatoes into a saucepan. Cover with water, add the salt, and boil for 7–10 minutes, until tender. Drain, then suspend the colander in the potato pan and cover with a clean tea towel for about 10 minutes, until the potatoes have steamed off and dried out a bit. Tip the spuds back into the pan, add the 10g/⅓oz of butter and mash until smooth. Cool slightly.

2. Pour the milk into a small saucepan. Add the sugar and 2 tablespoons of water and place it over a medium heat to warm up – you want it just warm.

3. In another pan, melt the 20g/⅔oz of butter over a medium heat. Add the flour and cook, stirring vigorously with a wooden spoon, for about 3 minutes, until the paste isn't sticking to the pan. Add the warm milk mixture little by little, stirring continuously, to form a smooth batter. Remove from the heat and beat in the egg until the mixture has cooled and it's gorgeously smooth.

4. Weigh out 200g/7oz of the cooled potato mixture (eat any extra) and add it into the batter in the pan. Beat together until fully combined.

5. Pour the oil into a large pan until about 7cm/3 inches deep. Place over a medium–high heat until it reaches 160–180°C/315–350°F on a cooking thermometer (or a bit of the potato mixture turns golden within 60 seconds).

6. While the oil is heating up, lightly dust your hands with flour and make 9 ping-pong-sized balls of the potato and choux dough.

7. About 3 at a time, fry the balls in the hot oil for 2–3 minutes, turning until golden and crispy. Drain each batch on kitchen paper while you fry the rest.

8. Spoon the chocolate spread into a piping bag (or sandwich bag) and snip the end to make a small opening. When the potato balls are cool enough to handle, use a skewer or cocktail stick to make a hole into the centre of each. Stick the piping bag into the holes and fill with some chocolate spread.

9. Spoon (or pipe) a splodge of Italian meringue on top of the buns and, if you have a kitchen blow torch, toast off the meringue for colour and texture. (If you don't have a blow torch, don't worry.) Serve 'em up to impress.

Simply the Zest Lemon Meringue Pie

Fun fact: I made this lemon meringue pie when my mates and I did a *Come Dine With Me* when we were sixteen. And I won. So you know it's good. I've loved a lemon meringue since I was a kid... and actually it may have been one of the first desserts I made. There's something about it that just makes me happy in every single way. Does anyone remember those packets of lemon meringue filling that you could buy? I loved nothing more than quickly whipping up my own pie and eating at least 80% of it myself. I will never get over the fact that something can be so sour, sweet, crunchy, fluffy and delightful all at one time. Top five desserts ever, in my eyes. Don't @ me.

Serves 6–8

The core
1 recipe quantity of **French or Italian Meringue** (see page 214 or 216)

For the pastry case
plain flour, for dusting
⅓ recipe quantity of **Sweet Pastry** (see page 182) or a shop-bought alternative

For the lemon curd
zest and juice of 4 **lemons**
2 tsp **cornflour** mixed with 2 tsp water to make a paste
200g/7oz **caster sugar**
110g/4oz **unsalted butter**, cubed, plus extra for greasing
4 **egg yolks**
1 **whole egg**

1. Grease a 23cm/9 inch loose-bottomed, fluted tart tin with a little butter.

2. Lightly dust your work surface with flour and roll out the pastry to a disc about 30cm/12 inches in diameter and 3mm/⅛ inch thick. Carefully transfer the disc to the tart tin and let it sink into the hollow. Gently press it into the corner around the base and up the side of the tin. Use a sharp knife to trim off any overhang.

3. Prick the base of the pastry case all over with a fork, then line it with a big piece of scrunched-up baking paper so that it covers the bottom and sides. Then, load up with baking beans or dried beans (see tip, page 120). Transfer it to the fridge to chill and rest for 30 minutes.

4. While the pastry case is chilling, preheat the oven to 190°C/170°C fan/ 375°F/Gas 5. Place a sieve over a bowl, ready to strain the curd.

5. Make the lemon curd. Place the lemon juice, cornflour paste and sugar in a medium saucepan over a medium–high heat. Bring to the boil, then boil for about 3 minutes, until it's thick and cloudy. Reduce the heat to low.

6. Add the butter a few cubes at a time, stirring as you go, and let it melt in.

7. Beat together the egg yolks and whole egg in a clean bowl. Add the lemony mixture in large spoonfuls to bring the eggs up to temperature (this will stop them scrambling when they go into the pan).

8. Add the egg mixture to the saucepan, stirring continuously as you do so. Cook over a low heat for about 10 minutes, until creamy and thick enough to coat the back of the spoon.

9. Pour the contents of the pan through the sieve into the bowl, pushing the curd through with the back of a spoon so that it's perfectly smooth in the bowl. Stir through the lemon zest and cover the surface of the curd with cling film (make sure it's actually touching the surface), which will stop a skin forming. Transfer to the fridge to cool.

10. Once the pastry has rested, blind bake the case for 15 minutes, until it's just browning, then remove the baking paper and beans and place the tart case back in the oven for a further 5 minutes, until golden on the base. Remove it from the oven and leave it to cool in the tart tin on a wire rack for about 10 minutes. (If you're using French meringue, leave the oven on.)

11. Load up the tart case with the cooled lemon curd.

12. Pipe or spoon on your meringue. If you are using French meringue, bake the pie for 15 minutes, or until slightly golden on top. If using Italian meringue, either kitchen blow torch it, or preheat the grill to medium and grill it for 5 minutes, until golden on top. Serve at room temperature.

SEE HOW IT SHOULD LOOK →

Index

A

ain't mushroom for lunch 144
almonds: cherry Bakewell cheesecake 194–7
anchovies: Caesar dressing 75
apples: apple mash 167
   apples 'n' pears pork 158
   butterscotch apple crumble 203
asparagus: greens means pasta 140–43
aubergine parmigiana 36
avocados: avo-bloomin-cado brunch wraps 60
   sweetcorn salsa 109

B

bacon: bacon-y garlic-y potato-y 48
   the breakfast salad 92–5
   brekkie quiche 127
   loaded potato salad 78
bananas and custard French toast 204
basil: pesto 63, 142–3
batter 102–17
   beer batter 106
   tempura batter 104
   Yorkshire puds 170
béarnaise sauce 80–83
béchamel sauce 40
   beef shin lasagne 50–53
   mac 'n' cheese 44
   Mrs Croque 47
beef: beef shin lasagne 50–53
   smoke and stout beef 160
   steak béarnaise 80–83
   stroganoff pie 132–5
   well-good meatballs 29
beer: smoke and stout beef 160
beer batter 106
   the DIY chippy dinner 114–17
   potato bhaji butty 113
black pudding: the breakfast salad 92–5
blind baking pastry 120, 193
Bombay potato pasties 128–31
bread: ain't mushroom for lunch 144
   croûtons 75, 94–5

flat breads 54–67
   a good pork stuffing 165
   honey parsnip crumble 171
   Mrs Croque 47
the breakfast salad 92–5
brekkie quiche 127
brioche: bananas and custard French toast 204
buffalo buttermilk chicken 98–9
burgers: potato bhaji butty 113
butter: butter-roasted carrots 173
   hollandaise 72
buttermilk: buffalo buttermilk chicken 98–9
butterscotch apple crumble 203

C

cabbage: tempura cabbage fritters 110
   see also red cabbage
Caesar dressing 75
capers: quick tartar sauce 116–17
caramel: forget-the-crème brûlées 210
carrots: apples 'n' pears pork 158
   beef shin lasagne 50–53
   butter-roasted carrots 173
   herb-roasted chicken 156
   smoke and stout beef 160
cauliflower le cheese 174
cheese: aubergine parmigiana 36
   avo-bloomin-cado brunch wraps 60
   beef shin lasagne 50–53
   brekkie quiche 127
   Caesar dressing 75
   cauliflower le cheese 174
   chicken parmigiana 34
   chilli garlic prawns and polenta 150
   halloumi, sweet potato and red onion salad 91
   Mrs Croque 47
   pesto 63, 142–3
   potato-topped pizza spud breads 63
cheese dressing 88
   blue cheese dressing 98–9
   feta dressing 96

cheese sauce 42
    bacon-y garlic-y potato-y 48
    cauliflower le cheese 174
    cheese and onion pie 122–5
cheesecake, cherry Bakewell 194–7
cherry Bakewell cheesecake 194–7
chicken: buffalo buttermilk chicken 98–9
    the chicken Caesar 75
    chicken parmigiana 34
    herb-roasted chicken 156
chilli garlic prawns and polenta 150
chips: crunchy roast chips 80–83
    the DIY chippy dinner 114–17
chocolate: s'mores dauphine 222
chorizo: popapas bravas 33
cider: apples 'n' pears pork 158
condensed milk: sweet potato pie
    190–93
confit garlic 136–51
    ain't mushroom for lunch 144
    chilli garlic prawns and polenta 150
    garlic-buttered crispy gnocchi
      146–9
    greens means pasta 140–3
coriander: avo-bloomin-cado brunch
    wraps 60
    Bombay potato pasties 128–31
    cucumber salad 59
corn-on-the-cob: buffalo buttermilk
    chicken 98–9
couscous 64–5
cream: Eton mess pancakes 221
    Pat's pav (on tour) 218
    perfect custard 200
crème brûlées 210
crème pat 186–7
croque madame 47
croûtons 75, 94–5
crumble: butterscotch apple
    crumble 203
    honey parsnip crumble 171
cucumber salad 59
curry: tikka salmon 59
custard 198–211
    bananas and custard French
      toast 204

butterscotch apple crumble 203
custard spudnuts 206–9
forget-the-crème brûlées 210
perfect custard 200

D
deep-frying 106
dip, soy 110
the DIY chippy dinner 114–17
doughnuts: custard spudnuts 206–9
dressings 84–101
    Caesar dressing 75
    cheese dressing 88
    vinaigrette dressing 87

E
easy flat breads *see* flat breads
eggs: the breakfast salad 92–5
    brekkie quiche 127
    eggs royale 76
    eggs shakshuka'd 30
    mayo 70
    Mrs Croque 47
emulsions 68–83
    hollandaise 72
    mayo 70
Eton mess pancakes 221

F
fish: the DIY chippy dinner 114–17
    eggs royale 76
    tikka salmon 59
flat breads 54–67
    avo-bloomin-cado brunch
      wraps 60
    easy flat breads 56
    potato-topped pizza spud breads 63
    slow-roasted harissa lamb
      shoulder 64–5
    tikka salmon 59
forget-the-crème brûlées 210
frangipane: cherry Bakewell
    cheesecake 194–7

French meringue 214
   Eton mess pancakes 221
   Pat's pav (on tour) 218
   simply the zest lemon meringue
     pie 224–7
French toast, bananas and custard 204
fritters, tempura cabbage 110

G
garlic: ain't mushroom for lunch 144
   apples 'n' pears pork 158
   bacon-y garlic-y potato-y 48
   chilli garlic prawns and polenta 150
   confit garlic 136–51
   garlic-buttered crispy gnocchi 146–9
   greens means pasta 140–3
   herb-roasted chicken 156
   smoke and stout beef 160
gherkins: quick tartar sauce 116–17
glaze, vanilla 208–9
gnocchi, garlic-buttered crispy 146–9
gravy 156, 160
greens means pasta 140–43

H
halloumi, sweet potato and red onion
   salad 91
ham: Mrs Croque 47
   well-good meatballs 29
harissa: slow-roasted harissa lamb
   shoulder 64–5
herb-roasted chicken 156
hollandaise 72
   eggs royale 76
   steak béarnaise 80–83
honey: cheat's honey glaze 47
   honey parsnip crumble 171
hot-sauce coating: buffalo buttermilk
   chicken 98–9

I
Italian meringue 216
   simply the zest lemon meringue
     pie 224–7
   s'mores dauphine 222

J
jam: Pop's pop tarts 188

K
kale: greens means pasta 140–43
kiwis: Pat's pav (on tour) 218

L
a labour of love *see* tomato sauce
lager: beer batter 106
lamb: slow-roasted harissa lamb
   shoulder 64–5
lasagne, beef shin 50–53
leeks: herb-roasted chicken 156
lemon: herb-roasted chicken 156
   lemon-roasted potatoes 96
   simply the zest lemon meringue
     pie 224–7
lettuce: buffalo buttermilk
   chicken 98–9
   the chicken Caesar 75
   halloumi, sweet potato and red
     onion salad 91
loaded potato salad 78

M
mac 'n' cheese 44
mangoes: Pat's pav (on tour) 218
marshmallows: sweet potato pie
   190–93
mascarpone: cherry Bakewell
   cheesecake 194–7
mayo 70
   the chicken Caesar 75
   loaded potato salad 78
   quick tartar sauce 116–17
meatballs 29
meringue 212–27
   Eton mess pancakes 221
   French meringue 214
   Italian meringue 216
   Pat's pav (on tour) 218
   simply the zest lemon meringue
     pie 224–7
   s'mores dauphine 222

milk: béchamel sauce 40
cheese sauce 42
crème pâtissière 186–7
mint: couscous 64–5
Mrs Croque 47
muffins: eggs royale 76
mushrooms: ain't mushroom for
lunch 144
brekkie quiche 127
stroganoff pie 132–5
well-good meatballs 29

O

olive oil: confit garlic 138
olives: couscous 64–5
onions: beef shin lasagne 50–53
cheese and onion pie 122–5
a good pork stuffing 165
halloumi, sweet potato and red
onion salad 91
herb-roasted chicken 156
potatoes boulangère 166
red onion tarte tatin 162
smoke and stout beef 160

P

pancakes, Eton mess 221
parma ham: well-good meatballs 29
parsley: ain't mushroom for lunch 144
chilli garlic prawns and polenta 150
couscous 64–5
parsnips: honey parsnip crumble 171
passion fruits: Pat's pav (on tour) 218
pasta: beef shin lasagne 50–53
greens means pasta 140–43
mac 'n' cheese 44
well-good meatballs 29
pasties, Bombay potato 128–31
pastry 180–97
blind baking 120, 193
savoury pastry 118–35
shortcrust pastry 120
pavlova: Pat's pav (on tour) 218
peanut butter: bananas and custard
French toast 204
pears: apples 'n' pears pork 158

peas: greens means pasta 140–43
pea salad 116–17
peppers: eggs shakshuka'd 30
greens means pasta 140–43
perfect custard 200
pesto 63, 142–3
pies: Bombay potato pasties 128–31
cheese and onion pie 122–5
simply the zest lemon meringue
pie 224–7
stroganoff pie 132–5
sweet potato pie 190–93
see also tarts
pine nuts: pesto 63, 142–3
pineapple: Pat's pav (on tour) 218
pizza spud breads, potato-topped 63
poached eggs 94–5
polenta, chilli garlic prawns and 150
pomegranate seeds: couscous 64–5
popapas bravas 33
Pop's pop tarts 188
pork: apples 'n' pears pork 158
a good pork stuffing 165
potatoes: apple mash 167
bacon-y garlic-y potato-y 48
Bombay potato pasties 128–31
the breakfast salad 92–5
crunchy roast chips 80–3
custard spudnuts 206–9
the DIY chippy dinner 114–17
garlic-buttered crispy
gnocchi 146–9
lemon-roasted potatoes with feta
dressing 96
loaded potato salad 78
popapas bravas 33
potato bhaji butty 113
potato-topped pizza spud
breads 63
potatoes boulangère 166
roast tatties 168
s'mores dauphine 222
prawns: chilli garlic prawns and
polenta 150
crispy prawn tacos 109

Q

quiche, brekkie 127

R

red cabbage: braised red cabbage 176
   buffalo buttermilk chicken 98–9
red onion tarte tatin 162
roasts 152–79
   apple mash 167
   apples 'n' pears pork 158
   butter-roasted carrots 173
   cauliflower le cheese 174
   a good pork stuffing 165
   herb-roasted chicken 156
   honey parsnip crumble 171
   potatoes boulangère 166
   red onion tarte tatin 162
   roast tatties 168
   smoke and stout beef 160
   Yorkshire puds 170

S

sage: garlic-buttered crispy
   gnocchi 146–9
salads: the breakfast salad 92–5
   buffalo buttermilk chicken 98–9
   the chicken Caesar 75
   cucumber salad 59
   halloumi, sweet potato and red
      onion salad 91
   loaded potato salad 78
   pea salad 116–17
salmon: tikka salmon 59
   see also smoked salmon
salsa, sweetcorn 109
sauces: béarnaise sauce 80–83
   béchamel sauce 40
   cheese sauce 42
   gravy 156, 160
   hollandaise 72
   perfect custard 200
   pesto 63, 142–3
   quick tartar sauce 116–17
   thickening 143
   tomato sauce 22–37
   white sauce 38–53
sausagemeat: a good pork
   stuffing 165
sausages: brekkie quiche 127
savoury pastry 118–35

shallots: loaded potato salad 78
shortcrust pastry 120
   Bombay potato pasties 128–31
   brekkie quiche 127
   cheese and onion pie 122–5
   stroganoff pie 132–5
simply the zest lemon meringue
   pie 224–7
smoke and stout beef 160
smoked salmon: eggs royale 76
s'mores dauphine 222
soffrito 50–53
soy dip 110
spaghetti: well-good meatballs 29
   see also pasta
spinach: Bombay potato pasties 128–31
   brekkie quiche 127
   chilli garlic prawns and polenta 150
spudnuts, custard 206–9
steak, testing for done-ness 82
steak béarnaise 80–83
stout: smoke and stout beef 160
strawberries: Eton mess pancakes 221
   strawberry tart 184–7
strawberry jam: Pop's pop tarts 188
stroganoff pie 132–5
stuffing, a good pork 165
sweet pastry 180–97
   cherry Bakewell cheesecake 194–7
   Pop's pop tarts 188
   simply the zest lemon meringue
      pie 224–7
   strawberry tart 184–7
   sweet potato pie 190–93
sweet potatoes: halloumi, sweet potato
   and red onion salad 91
   sweet potato pie 190–93
sweetcorn salsa 109

T

tacos, crispy prawn 109
tarragon: steak béarnaise 80–83
tartar sauce 116–17
tarts: Pop's pop tarts 188
   red onion tarte tatin 162
   strawberry tart 184–7
   see also pies

tempura batter 104
    crispy prawn tacos 109
    potato bhaji butty 113
    tempura cabbage fritters 110
thickening sauces 143
tikka salmon 59
toast: ain't mushroom for lunch 144
    bananas and custard French toast 204
tomato sauce 22–37
    aubergine parmigiana 36
    chicken parmigiana 34
    eggs shakshuka'd 30
    a labour of love 24
    popapas bravas 33
    the tomato quickie 26
    well-good meatballs 29
tomatoes: avo-bloomin-cado brunch
  wraps 60
    beef shin lasagne 50–53
    chilli garlic prawns and polenta 150
    potato-topped pizza spud breads 63
tortillas: crispy prawn tacos 109

V

vanilla: perfect custard 200
    vanilla glaze 208–9
vinaigrette dressing 87
    the breakfast salad 92–5
    halloumi, sweet potato and red
      onion salad 91

W

white sauce 38–53
    bacon-y garlic-y potato-y 48
    béchamel sauce 40
    beef shin lasagne 50–53
    cheese sauce 42
    mac 'n' cheese 44
    Mrs Croque 47
wine: beef shin lasagne 50–53
wraps, avo-bloomin-cado brunch 60

Y

yogurt: easy flat breads 56
Yorkshire puds 170

I say potato...

A big hello to everyone in North America! Or, as we say in Birmingham, England, where I'm from... 'How am ya bab?' You'll find measurement conversions throughout the book, but I know there are a few words that are a bit different over your way. For example, I spend a lot of time talking about an aubergine emoji and you're probably thinking... 'Huh?' To translate, I'm basically obsessing over an eggplant. Below, you'll find a list of Britishisms and what they relate to on your side of the Atlantic. Enjoy!

BRITISH	NORTH AMERICAN
Aubergine	Eggplant
Bacon lardons	Slab bacon sliced into matchsticks
Bap	Bread roll
Beef mince	Ground beef
Beef shin	Beef shank
Beef topside	Round roast/steak
Bicarbonate of soda	Baking soda
Caster sugar	Superfine sugar
cba	Can't be bothered
Chestnut mushrooms	Cremini mushrooms
Closed-cup mushrooms	White mushrooms
Coriander (fresh)	Cilantro (fresh)
Cornflour	Cornstarch
Double cream	Heavy/whipping cream
Flaked almonds	Slivered almonds
Gherkins	Dill pickles
Glacé cherries	Candied cherries
Gram flour	Chickpea flour
Grill	Broiler/broil
Icing sugar	Confectioners'/powdered sugar
Lashings	Lots of!
Maris piper potatoes	Russet potatoes
Piping bag	Pastry bag
Plain flour	All-purpose flour
Prawns	Shrimp
Punnet	Quart
Self-raising flour	A combination of all-purpose flour, baking powder and salt. Make your own with this ratio: 1 cup flour + 1½ tsp baking powder + ¼ tsp salt
Soured cream	Sour cream
Spring onions	Scallions/green onions
Tatties/spuds	Potatoes
Tomato purée	Tomato paste
White cabbage	Green cabbage

Thank You

I want to firstly thank everyone who has supported, followed, liked, shared everything or anything I've done over the last 12 months. Without you, this girl wouldn't have gone from being an unemployed chef to a PUBLISHED AUTHOR in just over a year. This is literally dream-come-true stuff. I wanted to make a book that my followers want and need, and I hope I've done that.

The book wouldn't have been a thing if it hadn't been for a little platform known as TikTok. It has definitely been a benefit having younger siblings and I want to say a massive thank you to my little brother Christian and little sister Trixie, who helped teach this old dog new tricks. If I can say one thing to you two directly, it's that having a recipe book has been an ambition of mine since I was your age, so I can't wait to see you guys rule the world and do whatever you set out to.

A big thank you to everyone at the publishers. First, Holly Jarrald for spotting my potential early on when I was just starting out. Then, Rowan Yapp for pushing it to the next level, Kitty Stogdon for breaking everything down for someone who didn't have a clue what was going on half the time (WTF is a DPS?!), Ellen Williams and Don Shanahan for making up the dream team getting the book in front of as many people as possible, and Judy Barratt for humouring my innuendos and inch knowledge, and understanding my boujee take on the English language. And that's not forgetting the incredible team across the seas who took a punt on this British girl! I feel very lucky to have gone through this process with such amazing people.

I couldn't have been happier working with an incredible team on the photoshoots and bringing to life everything in my head. Louise Hagger, who, with her assistant Sophie Bronze, meant that the photography was so strong that I was confident that even if I dropped the strawberry tart (which definitely didn't happen...), it'd still look amazing. Alexander Breeze, whose prop work has given me a new appreciation of tupperware and how it should be placed. Felix Neill for getting my vision and putting up with my pickiness over fonts. Can we have the next book in Comic Sans?

The biggest shout-out to two of the most talented, hardworking, understanding chefs I've worked with over the years – Siegfried Gatdula and Evelyn Wong. There's a reason I picked these two previous colleagues to help with food preparation on the shoot days and they did not disappoint. Fred – your attitude, work ethic and passion for food is going to see you go far and I can't wait to see where it takes you. Evelyn – one of the best pastry chefs I've ever had the pleasure to work with and your knowledge knows no bounds (can I have that brownie recipe again?).

I also had two very special people on set to help wash-up, prep veg and run to the supermarket again, again and again for everything I'd forgotten. Thanks to my mom Victoria Downing and my boyfriend's mom Rosie Shattock, for all your help on set. Moms really do save the day.

And finally, thank you to the best models in the business, who I was overwhelmed to have feature in my book. Kipper and Krypto, your pug modelling is unparalleled and I was honoured to have you on set for the day. When you weren't humping each other, you really did pull it out of the bag.

Their assistant, Tom Shattock, also helped a bit, too.

About Poppy

Poppy has spent a decade in professional kitchens – ranging from Michelin-starred restaurants and fine-dining experiences to kitchens serving tasty everyday food. In March 2020, while she was working as a junior sous chef at an exclusive members' club, the Covid-19 pandemic hit and she lost her job. She turned to TikTok as a creative outlet, and her educational and entertaining content led to more than a million followers in just over seven months. She shares the skills she's learnt from her time in the restaurant industry to inspire and teach people how to cook at home, from the very basics, right up to achievable restaurant-quality food – as well as a potato or two. Originally from near Birmingham, she now lives in East London with her boyfriend and two pugs. *Poppy Cooks: The Food You Need* is her first cookbook.

Find Poppy @poppycooks on TikTok and @poppy_cooks on Instagram.